Mediterranean Diet Air Fryer Cookbook

The Complete Air Fryer Cookbook for Beginners with Delicious, Easy & Healthy Mediterranean Diet Recipes to Lose Weight and Live a Healthy Lifestyle

contained within this document, including, but not limited to, —
errors, omissions, or inaccuracies.

Table of Contents

Air Fryer Tortellini with Prosciutto

Air Fryer Herb and Cheese-Stuffed Burger

Air Fryer Turkey Croquettes

Air Fryer Bourbon Bacon Cinnamon Rolls

Air Fryer Coconut Shrimp and Sauce

Air Fryer Quentin-Bourbon Feather

Chapter 6: Air Fried Mediterranean Snack Recipes

Air Fryer Pizza

Air Fried Vegetables

Baked General Tso's Cauliflower

Crispy Baked Avocado Tacos

Baked Potatoes

Air Fryer Potato Chips

Buttermilk Fried Mushroom

Chapter 7: Air Fried Mediterranean Dinner Recipes

Air Fryer Blacken Fish Tacos

Air Fryer Coconut Chicken

Air Fryer Salmon Patties

Breaded Air Fryer Pork Chops

Air Fryer BBQ Ribs

Mexican-Style Air Fryer Stuffed Chicken Breast

Air Fryer Beef Wellington

Easy Air Fryer Pizza

Quinoa Air Fried Burger

Air Fried Unsaturated Veggies

Chapter 1: An Introduction to The Mediterranean Diet

Congratulations on purchasing *Mediterranean Diet Air Fryer Cookbook* and thank you for doing so.

When you consider Mediterranean food, your mind may indulge in pizza and pasta from Italy, or lobe chops from Greece, but these dishes do not fit into healthy diet plans advertised as "Mediterranean". A real Mediterranean diet is provided with the traditional fruits of the region, vegetables, beans, nuts, seafood, olive oil, and dairy - perhaps a glass or two of wine. Therefore, residents of Crete, Greece, and southern Italy ate Circa in 1960, when their chronic disease rates around the world were among the rock bottom and, despite only limited medical services, they had great anticipation.

And the real Mediterranean diet is about eating fresh, nutritious food. Daily physical activity and sharing food with others are important elements of the Mediterranean diet pyramid. Together, they will have a profound effect on your mood and psychological state and will foster a deep appreciation for the pleasure of eating healthy and delicious foods.

Of course, making changes to your diet is never easy, especially if you are trying to do away with the convenience of processed and takeout foods. But the Mediterranean diet is often cheaper and satisfying to eat and healthier. Making the switch from pepperoni and pasta to fish and avocado may take some effort, but you'll soon be on your way to a healthier and longer life.

Health Benefits of the Mediterranean Diet

A traditional Mediterranean diet consisting of many fresh fruits and vegetables, nuts, fish and olive oil - combined with physical activity - can reduce the risk of great mental and physical health problems by you: heart condition and stroke.
Following a Mediterranean diet limits your intake of refined bread, processed foods, and meat, and encourages drinking instead of hard liquor - all factors that will help prevent heart conditions and strokes.

Keep you tight If you are an older adult, the nutrients obtained with the Mediterranean diet can reduce your risk of developing muscle weakness and other symptoms of waste by about 70 percent.

Reducing Alzheimer's risk. Research suggests that Mediterranean diets can improve cholesterol, blood sugar levels and overall vessel health, which can progressively reduce the risk of Alzheimer's disease or dementia.

Reducing the risk of Parkinson's disease. High levels of antioxidants within the Mediterranean diet can prevent cells from undergoing a harmful process called oxidative stress, reducing the risk of Parkinson's disease by half.

Increasing longevity. By reducing your risk of developing heart conditions or cancer with a Mediterranean diet, you are reducing your risk of death by 20% at any age.

Prevention from type 2 diabetes The Mediterranean diet is rich in fiber that digests slowly, prevents a massive drop in blood sugar and can help you maintain a healthy weight.

Myths and Facts about the Mediterranean Diet

There are many benefits to post-, but there are still many misconceptions on how to cash in on a healthy, long life to capitalize on a lifestyle. The following are some myths and facts about the Mediterranean diet.

Myth 1: This method costs tons to eat.
Fact: If you are making a meal out of beans or lentils as your main source of protein, and are mostly studded with plants and whole grains, the Mediterranean diet is more expensive than serving packaged or processed foods.

Myth 2: If one glass of wine is sweet for your heart, then three glasses are 3 times healthy.

Fact: A moderate amount of wine (one drink each day for women; two for men) certainly has unique health benefits for your heart, but drinking in excess has other effects. Anything quite two glasses of wine can be bad for your heart.

Myth 3: Eating large bowls of pasta and bread is the Mediterranean way.

Fact: Usually, the Mediterranean does not eat a huge plate of pasta the way Americans do. Instead, pasta is typically a funeral with some 1/2-cup to 1-cup serving sizes. The remainder of their plate consists of lettuce, vegetables, fish or organic, grass-fed meat and a slice of bread.

Myth 4: The Mediterranean diet is only about food.

Fact: Food can be a big part of the diet, yes, but do not ignore the opposite ways to live a Mediterranean life. Once they sit for a meal, they do not sit in front of a TV or dine in a hurry; They sit with others to have a relaxed, leisurely meal, which can be as important for your health as it is on your plate. The Mediterranean also enjoys many physical activities.

How to Make Changes

If you're feeling crazy thinking about adjusting, you're eating habits to a Mediterranean diet, here are some tips that urge you to start:

Eat many vegetables, vegetable oil and icing Try an easy plate of chopped tomatoes dripped with crumbled cheese, or add your thin-crust pies with peppers and mushrooms instead of sausage and pepperoni Load Ga. Salads, soups and crudité platters are also great for loading on vegetables.

Always have breakfast Fruits, whole grains, and other fiber-rich foods are excellent thanks to the start of your day, keeping you pleasantly plentiful for hours.

Eat seafood twice every week. Fishes such as tuna, salmon, herring, sablefish (black cod), and sardines are rich in omega-3 fatty acids and shellfish such as muscles, oysters, and clams have similar benefits for brain and heart health.

Cook a vegetarian meal one night every week. If this is useful, you will hope for a trend of eating meat on the primary day of the week or just pick a place every day where you cook meals around beans, whole grains, and vegetables. Once you get the hang of it, try two nights every week.

Enjoy dairy products carefully. The USDA recommends limiting saturated fat to a very low 10% of your daily calories (about 200 calories for many people). It also allows you to enjoy dairy products like natural (unprocessed) cheese, Greek or plain yogurt.

For dessert, eat fresh fruit. Instead of frozen sweets, cakes, or other food, choose strawberries, fresh figs, grapes, or apples.

Use good fat. Extra-virgin vegetable oils, nuts, sunflower seeds, olives, and avocados are great sources of healthy fats for your daily diet.

What to try about mercury in fish?
Despite all the health benefits of seafood, almost all fish and shellfish have traces of pollutants, including toxic metal mercury. These guidelines can help you make the safest choice.

The concentration of mercury and other pollutants increases in larger fish, so it is best to avoid eating large fish such as sharks, swordfish, tilefish, and caveolae.
Most adults can safely eat 12 ounces (two 6-ounce servings) of other types of cooked seafood every week.
Pay attention to local seafood advice to find out if the fish you caught is safe to eat.

For pregnant, nursing mothers, and young women ages 12 and younger, choose fish and shellfish that are low in mercury, such as shrimp, canned light tuna, salmon, pollock, or catfish. Due to its high mercury content, do not eat 6 ounces (an average meal) of albacore tuna per week.

Make mealtime a social experience. The simple act of lecturing a lover or loved one on the dining table can play a big role in relieving stress and boosting mood. Eating with others can also prevent overeating; it is as healthy for your waist as it is for your attitude. Cut out the TV and computer, remove your smartphone, and hook up with someone during the meal.

Gather the family together and yet be awake with each other's daily lives. Regular family meals provide comfort to children and is an excellent thanks for keeping an eye on their eating habits as well.

Share food with others to expand your social network. If you live alone, cook a touch extra and invite a boyfriend, coworker, or neighbor to join you.

Cook with others. Invite a lover to share shopping and cooking responsibilities for Mediterranean food. Cooking with others is often thanks to deepening relationships and dividing prices, it can be cheaper for both of you.

Quick Start for Mediterranean Diet Mediterranean Diet

The easiest thanks to making changes are to start with small steps. You will do this:

Cook in vegetable oil instead of butter.

Enjoying salads as a starter or Antrim, eating more fruits and vegetables, snacking on fruits, and incorporating veggies into other dishes.

Choosing whole grains instead of refined bread, rice, and pasta.

Replacement of fish at least twice per week for meat.

Limit high-fat dairy by turning 2% or milk to skim or 1% milk.

Try this Mediterranean alternative:

chips, pretzels, crackers and ranch dip carrots, celery, broccoli and soda with stir-fried meat. White rice with quinoa mustard fried vegetables with light bread sandwiches or whole-wheat sandwich stuffing with ice cream made with halwa skim or 1% milk tortillas.

The Mediterranean Diet (Mediate), abundant in minimally processed plant-based foods, rich in vegetable-rich monounsaturated fats, but low in saturated fats, meats, and dairy products, is an ideal nutritional model for heart health. Methods of Mediterranean intervention trials, limitations within the quality of some meta-analyzes, and other issues may have raised recent controversies. It is unclear whether such limitations are important to attract Med Diet's post cardiovascular benefits. We aimed to review the current evidence on the role of Mediate in heart health. We systematically searched for observable perspective correlations and randomized controlled trials that were explicitly reported to assess the effect of Media on hard cardiovascular endpoints. We critically evaluated all earlier cohorts and randomized controlled trials included within the 5 most comprehensive meta-analysis published between 2014 and 2018 and additional prospective studies were not included in these meta-analyses, with a total of 45 reports of prospective studies (4 32 independent observational groups) including randomized controlled trials. We addressed prevalent controversies on methodology and other issues. Some departures from individual randomization during membership of the Landmark Spanish trial (PREDIMED [Prevention con Diet Mediterranean]) did not represent any clinically meaningful attenuation within the strength of their findings, and therefore PREDIMED's results were robust across a wide selection of sensitivities. Analyze. Work-because standards were met, and potential sources of controversy did not represent any reason to compromise most findings of available observational studies and randomized controlled trials. The available evidence is large, strong, and consistent. Better congruence with general mediate is related to better heart health outcomes, including clinically meaningful reductions in rates of coronary heart status, ischemic stroke, and total disorder.

Diet is traditionally considered a key determinant of heart health. One of the 7 heart health metrics proposed in 2010 by the American Heart Association (Simple 7 of Life) directly matches a healthy diet. But at the same time, the remaining 6 proposed health metrics (body mass index, vital signs, total cholesterol, and blood sugar) are closely determined by the other 4 dietary habits. Also, another health metric, physical activity, represents the exact opposite side of the energy balance equation and is indirectly associated with dietary energy intake. Therefore, a healthy diet is important to meet most of life's simple 7 goals and to ensure heart health.

In this context, the general quality of whole food patterns may be more important and more interpretable than analyzes focused on single nutrients or foods. The study of overall food patterns represents the current state of the art within the investigation of nutritional determinants of heart health. This approach is advantageous because it confounds different dietary factors and it captures the synergistic effects of different foods and nutrients. It is also going to provide a more powerful tool to assess the effect of dietary habits on heart health as the effect of a dietary element being too small to be detected in epidemiological studies or randomized controlled trials (RCTs) is. On the contrary, it seems logical that the cumulative effect of many different aspects of the diet is probably going to be quite large.

The Mediterranean Diet (Med Diet) represents an overall holistic dietary pattern in nutritional epidemiology that has been extensively studied, especially during the last 2 decades.

Med Diet is defined as a standard eating pattern found among populations living within the Mediterranean basin during the 50th and 60th centuries, but, unfortunately, not today. Meditates most characteristic at the time was a coffee consumption of meat and meat products, with very little consumption of meat (beef, pork, and lamb were reserved for special occasions only), processed meats, and very little butter. Or null consumption, ice cream, or other whole-fat dairy products (only fermented dairy products, cheese, and yogurt, consumed in moderate amounts). It presents a comparatively fat-rich profile due to the abundant consumption of vegetable oil, with high consumption of locally grown vegetables, fruits, nuts, legumes, and grains (mainly unrefined). 6 Protein Was an important source of A moderate consumption of fish and shellfish, which was variable counting at the proximity of the sea. Most sources of fat and alcohol among individuals within the traditional meditate are mainly extra virgin vegetable oil (EVOO) and alcohol, respectively. The abundant use of vegetable oil, along with salads, traditionally cooked vegetables and legumes, along with moderate consumption of wine during meals make this diet highly nutritious and tasty. Vines and EVOOs contain many bioactive polyphenols, oleocanthal, and resveratrol) with many anti-inflammatory properties. The post-antimicrobial properties of vegetable oil were reportedly attributed to the high content of monounsaturated fat (MUFA; oleic acid) and some new investigations also suggest that bioactive polyphenols are present only within EVOO, but vegetable oil Not within the sophisticated-common type of. May contribute to those cardioprotective functions. EVOO is the primary pressure product of black olive fruit and contains many antioxidants (polyphenols, tocopherols, and phytosterols). Low-quality oils (refined or common olive oil) are believed to be barren of most of those antioxidant, anti-inflammatory or pulmonary abilities as they are obtained by physical and chemical processes that contain fat but most of the bioactive Elements cause damage.

In the Spanish Landmark PREDIMED trial (Prevenient con data Mediterranean), which freed 7447 high-risk participants initially from the disorder (CVD), a 5-year intervention with Mediate significantly reduced the occurrence of an overall major CVD endpoint Which included non-fatal strokes. , Non-coronary heart condition (CHD), and every single fatal CVD event. However, the results of that test were recently withdrawn by S and simultaneously republished in the same journal. He included several new analyzes and addressed some of the smaller departures from individual randomization more broadly. Despite this, many questions remain as to whether Mediate can provide benefits for heart health in both Mediterranean and non-Mediterranean populations. It is also uncertain how variations within the components of the Mediate index used in various studies may affect this association. Additionally, other possible sources of bias must be adequately addressed.

In the first sections of this lesson, we will discuss some potential concerns about the beneficial cardiovascular effects of the Med Diet. Within the following sections, we will address the issues associated with these concerns. Currently, available evidence strongly supports Meditate as an ideal approach to heart health.

Possible limitations associated with the concept and operational definitions of

Med Diet an idea promoted primarily or partly for geo-romantic-indifferent reasons?

Many of the investigators who are currently strong supporters of Meditate have originated, lived, or have ancestry in Mediterranean countries. This may be a cause for concern as they would be biased when selecting pieces of evidence that best slot into the image of their prior perceptions of what a healthy diet should be. They are likely to include those aspects of their diet that they have loved since childhood and even learned from their grandparents or ancestors. It is easy to think that there may be a kind of mixture of scientific and fruitless reasons, many of them unconscious, during this group of investigators and these mixed motives may have contributed to their strong positions and opinions on cardiovascular benefits. Of meditate. This claim, as discussed below, does not support the fact that many studies conducted in non-Mediterranean populations have found similar benefits of Mediterranean-type dietary patterns on CVD risk.

Is the Meditate idea supported by the vested business interests of vegetable oil and nuts companies?

The potential bias in biomedical investigations involving research funding by the pharmaceutical industry is largely studied and documented. It is well known that there is a large correlation between industry sponsorship and pro-industry findings. But similar biases associated with research funding by the food industry are only recently documented. Pro-industry bias in pharmaceutical research may have adverse health effects on many patients receiving medications, but in nutritional research, the pro-industry bias may be adverse health for all, with a substantial loss to public health. Will affect. Additionally, regulations for drug research are strict for nutrition research.

The scientific truth in the wilderness of academia — nothing more, nothing less — should be the first objective that everyone should pursue. This statement has often been repeated within the scientific environment surrounding investigators on nutrition and heart health. The first interest of multinational food companies is to expand their profits, and consequently, to make profitable food choices easier. Conversely, the first interest of public health is to make healthier choices easier. There is a transparent conflict of interest. Several published studies, particularly small trials with soft endpoints and reviews or comments on the advantages of Mediate for heart health, are funded by food industries or were written after their presentation at an industry-funded meeting. Although there is not a uniform range compared to sugar-sweetened beverages, this potential conflict of interest has been criticized, particularly about the concept of Mediate. BMJ's previous editor, Richard Smith, wrote, "A combination of vested interests, including the International Vegetable Oil Council and a PR company Old way, which promoted the diet, combined the diet with the natural charm of the Mediterranean." Popular ". However, these criticisms do not stand and support the fact that much of the evidence on Meditate has been publicly funded. We will discuss this issue during a later section.

Should refined grains be treated as mediate neighbors?
Currently available epidemiological evidence to consume less frequent refined grains and replace them by whole grain They support the advice. This replacement will reduce the risk of type 2 DM and CVD. However, within Mudit's most used operational definition, all grains are included as a positive item. There is no difference between refined and whole-grain grains. The idea that each one grain, including refined grains, provides cardiovascular protection, is the current scientific method. May be against the values. Modified the score developed by Trichoplax and included

only whole grain products within the Alternative Mediterranean Diet (Immediate) score.

Similarly, Panagiotis get much of the Mediate for very good consumption of whole grains. Followed by more. This modification seems more in line with current mainstream findings in nutritional science. The PREDIMED trial did not include grain consumption within the Meredith rearing regimen. This difference may make one suspect the reliability of some Mudit scores for capturing dietary patterns with the most significant potential for cardiovascular health.

Can alcohol still be a part of Mediate?

A moderate intake of alcohol is generally considered a positive item in most of the Mediate index. However, the results of a recent study have simultaneously acknowledged alcohol consumption as the major factor of the global disease burden. There is a view — based on some studies with inherent limitations — that alcohol, whenever moderately consumed, increases the risk of many diseases. A dose-response relationship probably exists between alcohol and various types of cancer. For this reason, some optimized Mudit scores excluded alcohol intake to assess the association between Mediate and carcinoma adherence. Thus, there is a question as to whether moderate alcohol consumption should not be used in the Meditates operational definition. Moderate consumption of alcohol with food is considered one of the components of Mediate, as discussed below, although alcohol intake is not encouraged for those who do not drink alcohol.

Do dairy products play any role within Med Diet?
The role of dairy products in cardiovascular health is controversial. However, for some dairy products, particularly fermented dairy products, metabolic benefits are reported during a nonspecific relationship, and a meta-analysis found significant reductions in the incidence of stroke-related to food consumption. Nevertheless, all dairy products are negatively weighted within the Mediate score proposed by Hristopoulos. However, those following amide and, therefore, Med Diet adherence excluded most dairy products with a null value. This is another source of discrepancy between the points often used in various studies that contribute to the idea that Mediate may be a broad term that varies in the literature.

Are Potatoes and Eggs a Neighborhood of Mediated Definition?
In all those definitions, potatoes were excluded from the vegetable group when calculating the mediate score. But potatoes with a smaller number of vegetables were included during the score, such as those employed by Tegan et al. And by Mozette et al. In the other 2 reports, they were positively weighted (supposedly beneficial) as they were included with grains.

Typically, egg consumption is not included in the definitions of meditation, but some studies included negative weight gain with meat or egg intake as a separate item.

Historical observational studies have previously noted that relating to mediate with cardiovascular mortality, 22S explicitly stated that potatoes and eggs should be kept separate from the rating system for the mediate, and thus received a zero consideration.

Should any diet rich in fruits and vegetables be the standard mediate?

Surprisingly, some meta-analyses categorized any Mediterranean dietary pattern as meeting a minimum of 2 criteria out of seven. The rationale for these criteria is quite controversial and this terminology is misleading because it means, for example, that any diet rich in fruits and vegetables can be called a Mediterranean-style diet.

What are the most sources of fat and fat subtypes within the Med Diet?

In the most common definition of Med Diet, the MUFA: saturated fat (SFA) ratio is one of 9 that wants to construct a score, but other scores have used it instead of unsaturated: SFA ratio, which includes polyunsaturated fat, which Much is attributed to the fact. Other sources of MUFA aside from vegetable oil are generally important in non-Mediterranean regions and so are the common finding of beneficial cardiovascular effects when SFA is replaced by fat. In other Mediterranean scores, instead of using the MUFA: SFA ratio, only vegetable oil consumption was selected for this item. Although vegetable oil will not correspond to the most important source of fat for heart health, the use of vegetable oil as the main culinary fat is an important feature of meditation. The PREDIMED trial gave EVOO a special significance as a source of bioactive polyphenols. These polyphenols are increasingly noted for cardiovascular health benefits due to their anti-inflammatory properties. Interestingly, the 14-item questionnaire used in PREDIMED was during an ll. Among each a> score that captured a very good intake of polyphenol antioxidant content compared to 21 Mediatizes.

Are polyphenols enough for a significant effect?
There are differences between the Mediterranean and non-Mediterranean countries regarding the types of flavonoids and food sources. But when a high polyphenol content of mediate is thought to be partially responsible for the cardiovascular benefits of this food pattern, a relevant question is usually raised: what is the minimum number of bioactive polyphenols, which yield meaningful clinical results but sufficiently large will increase the pulmonary effect. effect? The total polyphenol urinary excretion between substitutions of PREDIMED was measured and therefore the lower turtle upper limit of excretion was equal to 32 mg of acid per gram of creatinine. How is it possible that these

polyphenols, which are present only in minuscule amounts, may also make up for a powerful reduction in cardiovascular clinical events? This quantitative question that was important when postulating resveratrol because the main element responsible for the potential protective effect of wine has not been adequately investigated in terms of the entire number of polyphenols present within specific foods of Medicaid. However, polyphenols are a neighborhood of synergy between several beneficial bioactive compounds within the mediate.

Are sample-specific cutoff scores used to score certain median scores?

The general approach to achieving multiple adherence for Med Diet is to use the sample-specific mean of each food group's consumption and to specify a point for items that are at or above the sex-specific median of the sample for the item Huh. Consistent with the concept of common mediate. Conversely, a point is given to participants who are below the sex-specific mean of consumption for items related to general mediate. In other figures, sample medians used textiles instead of using bifurcation.

Indo-Mediterranean Trial Rare Reliability Indo-Mediterranean Trial Lancet

published in 2002,98 results, resulting in a dramatic decrease in the incidence of cardiovascular outcomes in 499 patients on a diet rich in whole grains, fruits, vegetables, and walnuts. Compared to 501 controls allocated to the consumption of a field diet like almonds, a low-fat Phase I National Cholesterol Education Program diet. But later, in 2005, Lancet issued an expression of concern over the failure to locate the original research record. While this study has occasionally featured in both narrative and systematic reviews, it has been largely maligned and should be regarded as at least a critically flawed investigation.

Deviations from individual randomization protocols within the prescribed test The

Spanish PREDIMED trial included 7447 participants at high cardiovascular risk assigned to 1 of three diets: Medium supplemented with EVO, medicated supplemented with mixed nuts, or an impact diet (back Advice to scale) all subtypes of dietary fat). The trial was planned for six years, but it closed early after intervention for 4.8 years, as recommended by the Information and Security Monitoring Board because withholding regulations established a priority within the protocol. The incidence of CVD (MI, stroke, or cardiac death, a total of 288 events) within the Med Diet groups was 30% lower than in the control regimen.

Enrollment of household members (partner of a previous participant) without randomization; Random participants' household members were invited to participate and were allocated to a similar intervention group as their relatives. The second enrolled partners of the previous partner represented 5.7% of PREDIMED participants with a lower proportion in the control group (4.82%) than in the Minivet group + EVOO (6.72%) or Meditate group + nuts (5.54%). This was done to avoid assigning different diets to members of a different household. Handing over an equivalent diet to all participants in the household was the best way to realize diet changes within the home. This process was inadvertently left within the reporting of the protocol and, therefore, the original publication.

Baseline imbalance was slight and only included during a slightly higher percentage of girls within the control group (5.7% on top of things compared to the Mediate + Nuts group and 1% more on top of things than the Mediate + Ewe group) Within Med Diet + EVOO a 5.3% higher percentage of patients with higher levels of LDL-C (low-density lipoprotein cholesterol) within the control group. Interestingly, both are working against the hypothesis of litigation in either case and thus, this conclusion cannot provide any alternative non-explanatory description of the findings. Several criticisms were raised after the protocol revealed these departures.

The investigators of PREDIMED decided to withdraw their origin. And simultaneously republished a replacement addition within the same journal, where these issues were fully addressed.

The resurgence included results from several new sensitivity and ancillary analyzes that showed no change in terms of earlier results of PRIMED.

Strengths of the Mediterranean Diet

All previous considerations represent potential and pitfalls that threaten the validity of the Med Diet paradigm for heart health. There are also several strengths within the currently available evidence to support the validity of the proposal defending the Mediate model as it is an ideal approach to heart health.

Med Diet possesses a millennial tradition of use with no evidence of harm. Meditates current definitions are consistent with traditional food patterns during the 50s and 60s of the last century in the Mediterranean, where life expectancies after 45 years were among the best on the planet.

The pioneering epidemiological study supporting Meditate for heart health was not conducted within the Mediterranean region or by anyone living with Mediterranean ancestry. These first pieces of evidence came from studies in seven countries, and ecological, international, dietary investigation, and disorder in a total group of about 13 000 men in 7 countries (Greece, Italy, Japan, Finland, last Yugoslavia, the Netherlands, and) Were. Hence the United States). The study was started in 1958 by an

American investigator. It was he who developed and promoted the concept of cardioprotective mediate for the primary time. Therefore, it is unlikely that geographical-egocentric-romantic motivations associated with diet learned by some investigators in childhood from their grandparents may be based on this idea. Keynes was a physicist and epidemiologist at the University of Minnesota who discovered the mediates cardiovascular health benefits in the early 1950s, as a scientist about the rapidly increasing trend of coronary mortality within the Mediterranean. Countries visited. Keys did his first research on Mediate by studying men's dietary patterns and heart health in Italy, Spain, and Crete, with emphasis on dietary fat and fatty acid results on serum cholesterol levels and CVD risk. Their findings were particularly prominent regarding the importance of fat subtypes — and not total fat intake — and the relevance of the MUFA: SFA ratio. Meditate is relatively rich in fat (even up to 40% of calorie levels from fat), but with an optimal MUFA: SFA ratio appeared as an ideal model for heart health. These facts were by the long-standing experience of using this dietary pattern in relatively poor areas of the planet with high rates of smoking, and yet, with very low-CHD mortality.

Dietary pattern paradigms have several advantages. In contrast to the classical analytical approach of estimating exposure only for single nutrients or isolated foods, the study of overall dietary patterns has become the current prevailing framework in nutrition research. This approach has been fully adopted and supported by the 2015 Dietary Guidelines Advisory Committee. The pattern of food approach is beneficial for several reasons: because they can have synergistic or antagonistic effects after intake in combination with foods and nutrients; Composite eating patterns represent current practices found within current populations (people do not eat individual nutrients) and, therefore, they better capture particular risks of interest; They supply useful sociological information of great interest to public health in their own right; Use of dietary patterns because the relevant risk in nutrition reduces the ability to be confused by other dietary risks; And very importantly, the main goal on normal eating patterns seems to be superior to the reduces and all effects are attributed to one nutrient or food. It may seem unlikely that a single nutrient or food can have a sufficiently strong effect to alter rates of cardiac outcomes. Conversely, the summative effect of small changes in many foods and nutrients has a more biologically measurable and clinically meaningful effect. In fact, during the last 2 decades, several well-conducted prospective epidemiological studies have confirmed a strong relationship between a primary defined high-quality dietary pattern and a low risk of chronic disease, including cardiac clinical outcomes.

History of the Mediterranean Diet

The Mediterranean diet originates within the edible cultures of ancient civilizations, which evolved as the Mediterranean basin and vegetable oils (as the most sources of excess fat), plant foods (grains, fruits, vegetables, legumes, tree nuts) Is based on regular intake. , And seeds), balanced consumption of fish and seafood and dairy, and moderate-to-moderate alcohol (mostly red wine) intake by relatively limited use of meat and other meat products. A few decades ago, the Mediterranean diet attracted the eyes of medical professionals by offering expanded health benefits. The primary report explored cardiovascular protection, as several large-scale clinical studies, beginning with the Ansel Keys 'Seven Countries Study', showed a significant decrease in atherosclerotic clinical events in populations with Mediterranean dietary patterns. Forthcoming trials confirmed favorable effects on the risk of metabolic syndrome, obesity, type 2 DM, cancer, and neurodegenerative diseases. While its health benefits are universally recognized by medical professionals today, this state of the Mediterranean diet is challenged with great difficulties in applying this protective dietary pattern to other geographic and cultural regions and surviving it in the traditional Mediterranean Is kept, which is also affected by unhealthy eating. Habits brought by pronunciation around the world.

Traditional eating habits observed in geographic areas around the Mediterranean Sea, although differentiated by certain food choices and cooking practices specific to every country and culture, share a standard set of basic amenities. The exact dietary dimension of the Mediterranean lifestyle includes plant-based dishes using vegetable, vegetable, cereal, nuts, and legumes, most of which are cooked by adding substantial amounts of vegetable oil, with moderate use of fish, seafood, or dairy.

And limited intake of meat and alcohol (mostly wines). This unique dietary pattern came to be the result of a posh and multi-millennium interaction between natural food resources available within the Mediterranean environment and, therefore, the human element living in the Mediterranean basin throughout history. Become a precious medical device within the contemporary world within the last century

The combination of the term "Mediterranean Diet" and its success in the eyes of the medical public was made possible by the work of Ansel Keys, an American scientist. Primary to note the association between some traditional Mediterranean communities and the low incidence of the disorder in their specific dietary habits. Upcoming research confirmed the benefits by Mediterranean-derived dietary interventions not only within primary and secondary prevention of disorganization, but also within therapeutic approaches to obesity, type 2 diabetes, metabolic syndrome, cancer, or neurodegenerative diseases.

At a time when the recognition of the health benefits related to the Mediterranean diet has become universal, its irony is that its homeland areas are in danger of being extinguished. Globalization, the importation of Western habits, changes in lifestyles and therefore an environment specific to modern civilization have brought a significant toll on the general Mediterranean diet. At an equivalent time, when international guidelines include it in recommended healthy dietary patterns, the United Nations Educational, Scientific and Cultural Organization (UNESCO) considers the Mediterranean diet to be "the intangible cultural heritage of intensive protection". Given this conflicting stance between universal medical recognition and cultural extinction, the purpose of this paper is to review current information related to the establishment and development of the Mediterranean diet, the main medical evidence supporting its health benefits, and hence the challenges It has to be uprooted. To avoid erosion, to take care of survival and stability, and to serve public health with the simplest resources it can provide.

The term "Mediterranean diet" is employed today to explain the general dietary habits of neighboring countries of the Mediterranean, mostly Greece and southern Italy. Nevertheless, it should be understood to be quite strict about the preferences that these populations have displayed in their daily food selection because the first meaning of the word death in Greek is not just asking for food or food choices, but in a particular way. "living" better matches the fashionable concept of lifestyle.

The "Mediterranean point to the beginning of the diet is relatively hard, but the civilization morning basin, along with the outlandish population, has most likely evolved. Throughout history, the Mediterranean diet incorporated many of the habits brought by the conqueror, while keeping most of the previous local traditions alive and functional. The roots of the Mediterranean diet can also be found in ancient societies related to the Fertile Crescent - the Middle East geographic region that is the eastern end of the Mediterranean Sector Ice level position and therefore Mesopotamia, the Persian Gulf, including Canaan, and is consistent with northern Egypt.

The oldest of the Mediterranean foods among the basin countries and cultures. Hieroglyphic wine from Canaan records of ancient Egypt and olive exports are mentioned. The city-state of Athens depicted a fruit tree as its symbol, and so the ancient Greeks abandoned the offer of peace to humanity as an offering to peace. The Greek food influence was brought within the Middle East after Alexander conquered the region within the 4th century BC. As a plant-based diet, the Mediterranean diet received a sequential effect, as successive vegetation species were imported from other countries of the planet and acclimatized within the Mediterranean basin.

Food patterns on the Mediterranean coast were largely influenced by three main monotheistic beliefs that succeeded during the region: Judaism, Christianity, and Islam. These religions also adopted, kept alive, and held many of the essential components of the Mediterranean lifestyle as sacred.

The Mediterranean diet is not, in fact, a singular diet within the meaning of the word "diet". Each region within the Mediterranean basin developed its cuisine, preferences, and restrictions. The term "Mediterranean diet" can be understood as a specific "dietary pattern", in which specific characteristics are interrelated. Including certain foods contained within popular culture, ignoring the absence of other traditional foods or allowing the addition of foods related to other food cultures and patterns, should not be accepted as valid versions of the Mediterranean diet. An authentic Mediterranean dietary pattern should be viewed holistically, including all its characteristics, not just one of their neighborhoods. First, vegetable oil plays a central role within the cooking process, and thus, represents the most source of dietary fat. Cheese is employed in limited servings and usually within salads. Meat, milk, and eggs are consumed at a coffee frequency and in small quantities, and processed meat and sweets are practically non-existent. The Mediterranean diet, therefore, represents, in fact, the only traditional dietary pattern where consumption of saturated and trans fats is inherently minimal. Second, the consumption of vegetable oil is related to a better vegetable meal, cooked as a salad, and thermally prepared foods with an equally high beam intake, which means that the Mediterranean diet is a plant- Based dietary pattern. Other major components of the Mediterranean diet are whole grains, nuts, fresh fruits, and moderate fish intake. Grapes and their derivative products are also used, but one of the most characteristic features of the Mediterranean diet is that limited intake of alcohol, alcohol intake only with food, in small servings, with limited frequency throughout the week, and is done with consumption. Other alcoholic beverages such as alcohol or beer are not part of the normal lifestyle. However, some changes in food intake exist between different countries. For example, whole fat consumption varies substantially between Greece, where 40% or more of the entire daily calorie intake reaches a high figure, and Italy, where fat intake is up to 30% of daily calories, Is limited to moderate consumption. The consistent feature between different regions of the Mediterranean basin is the high proportion of monounsaturated to saturated fats, far exceeding the same proportion in Northern Europe or North America. Differences between countries also occur within the selection of other food sources. The Italian diet has superior pasta consumption, while the Spanish version of the Mediterranean diet features high fish and seafood. A literature review considering the differences between countries with a Mediterranean diet found that different from one case, three to nine vegetable servings, half to 2 fruit servings, from one to thirteen-grain servings, and eight vegetable oil combinations. Till every day. Although the amount of nutrients appears to vary, the number of different food servings, in most cases, substitutes for the different food groups complement each other, supplying the general unitary characteristics described above.

Studies and Research on the Mediterranean Diet

As a result of such geographic variations in food selection, diverse combinations of food groups are considered by current guidelines to create Mediterranean dietary patterns. The Diet Pyramid (a graphic representation of most principles within the diet, where foods allowed in large quantities are represented within the lower floors of the pyramid and restricted foods are pointed toward its top) to explain a Mediterranean diet today There are three main forms for Old ways Conservation and Exchange Trust Pyramid, Greek Nutritional Guidelines of the Common Mediterranean Diet, and Us Therefore Mediterranean Diet Foundation Pyramid. A number of these models maintained the characteristics of normal eating habits, while others were modified in time to increase suit supplies, food supplies, nutritional needs, and eating habits nowadays.

Ansel Keys is the person responsible for considering the health safety effects of the Mediterranean lifestyle and coining the term "Mediterranean diet". An expert in biology and animal physiology, Key focused on the physical body at the helm of Star Wars II, examining nutrition techniques designed to restore health after starvation. While specializing in starvation, the figures of morbidity and mortality in post-war Europe came under his eyes. He was surprised to note the main decline by acute coronary attacks in countries where famine led populations to limit their specific high-fat, high-calorie diet, and reversal trend when an equal country recovered after the war Happened and so the population changed feeding again. At an equivalent time, Keys became aware of a high incidence of heart attacks in middle-aged business people thriving within the US, when he suspected that diet may affect health and is particularly at risk for the disorder. During an era when the concept of risk factors had not yet arisen, the discovery study on heart conditions in Minnesota merchants was planned to become the primary prospective study on the disorder in the medical record.

While working at Oxford during a year's rest in 1951, he came to Southern Italy to hear of a very rare occurrence of a heart condition. Keys visited Naples and opened a transportable laboratory there. He soon agreed to corroborate previously heard stories about a low incidence of coronary ischemic disease and showed low cholesterol levels, which the locals had demonstrated. Key made similar evaluations in other European and African countries, gradually finding that diets rich in saturated fats were related to increased serum cholesterol levels and a higher risk for a coronary heart condition.

When Ansel Keyes first presented his dietary ideas on the condition of the heart at the World Health Organization's World Meeting in 1955, he was skeptical and challenged by world-renowned cardiologist Sir George Pickering to present additional evidence. Granted. Unable to do so for the immediate, he took it as an inspiration for style and implemented a search project that was to become the study of the so-called Seven Countries. They combined tobacco use, diet, physical activity, weight status, vital signs, pulse, lung capacity, blood cholesterol levels and electrocardiographic readings consisting of all men aged 40 to 59 at seven cohorts, a select few Live-in rural areas. Former Yugoslavia, Italy, Greece, Finland, Netherlands, US, and Japan. Yugoslavia was chosen to offer the possibility to review populations in the coastal and inland regions of the country with two different eating patterns. Italy was the country where Ansel Keys made his initial remarks on the low incidence of heart conditions within the setting of a distinct (albeit not yet named) Mediterranean lifestyle. Greece offered an opportunity to scale up the population with a high-fat diet, but with a low intake of saturated fat, as the main source of fat was vegetable oil containing monounsaturated fatty acids. Finland's population was well-off but exhibits a high incidence of heart disease and a high intake of saturated fat sources. The Netherlands was representative of a moderate dietary pattern, with mixed consumption of meat, butter, and vegetables. The US population sample was chosen as representative of the incidence of the high disorder and for its geographic stability over time. Japan offered the possibility to review the population with a diet with minimum dietary fat. A total of 12,763 subjects were screened. At 5 and 10 years, respectively, the study team returned to all or any of the populations that were initially investigated and picked up data about participants who had meanwhile experienced a coronary attack.

When medical data was presented for statistical analysis, the results showed significant differences between geographic regions. During this sequence, rock bottom rates were found in attack events in Crete, Japan, and Corfu. On the opposite end of the spectrum, very good rates were identified in Finland, with the US ranking second.

Direct comparisons between Crete and Finland showed the incidence of coronary attacks to be approximately 100 times higher within the latter (0.1% compared to 9.5%). Seventeen percent of Finnish had total cholesterol levels above 200 mg/dl, compared to only seventy percent Japanese. Dietary calories derived from total fat varied between 9% and 40% of the total daily intake, but these data were not always related to the occurrence of heart conditions, as Greece had the best total fat intake. Calories derived from saturated fat vary between 3% and

22%; The correspondence between the incidence of heart attack and saturated fat was convincing. Excess intake of saturated fat was documented to be related to an improved incidence of the disorder in Finland and our communities.

The study of seven countries had an observational design and limited power to demonstrate a cause-effect relationship. Keyes and his team became condensed on the association between total serum cholesterol levels and, therefore, the dietary factors affecting them, on the possibility that the Mediterranean dietary pattern had a beneficial effect on whole heart health. Although the intake countries study pointed to the connections that exist between eating habits and cardiovascular risk, the concept of a "Mediterranean diet" was kept within the background until the early 1990s.

The Lyon Diet Heart Study was a secondary prevention randomized controlled trial to assess the results of a contemporary, French-adapted version of the Mediterranean diet in patients already suffering from an acute myocardial infarction. Therefore, mimicking the characteristics of the Greek diet is naturally rich in omega-3 fatty acids, but poor in omega-6 linolenic acid, S decided to use rape oil with vegetable oil. As some surprise, the results of this research not only showed a 50% reduction of the latest acute coronary episodes but also discounted the number of latest cancer cases and all-cause mortality. The health benefits of the Mediterranean eating style can no longer be ignored, and so the concept of the "Mediterranean diet" entered the medical consciousness.

In the following years, the cardinal benefits of the Mediterranean diet became stronger. At the time of recruitment, 74,607 healthy participants from nine European countries, aged 60 or older, did not include a variant of the Mediterranean Diet Score, within the AQ Prospective Investigation (EPIC) Large Cooperation in Cancer and Nutrition (EPIC). To estimate adherence to the Mediterranean diet. The score was obtained by adding nine partials multiple 0s or 1s, representing the intake of nine specific dietary components, and thus varying between absolute 0 (lowest adherence) and 9 (highest adherence). After a 4-year follow-up, a 2-point increase within the values of this Mediterranean diet score was found to be related to a 33% decrease in cardiac death. Two other Spanish cohort studies, also because the Multinational Healthy Aging: A Longitudinal Study (HELL) project in Europe, confirm the association between better adherence to the Mediterranean diet and a lower number of cardiac events, also in primary prevention settings. A relaxation in heart incidence rate was also observed in several secondary prevention studies.

One of the more recent large trials to supply strong evidence in favor of the Mediterranean diet was the Spanish Prevention con diet Mediterranean (PREDIMED) study. Designed as a controlled randomized trial as the primary prevention, it enrolled 7447 subjects with no clinical signs of abstinence, including those advised to follow a diet group, and extra-virgin vegetable oil or Two active experimental groups were determined to follow a Mediterranean diet supplemented with mixed nuts. Although all three groups showed a small number of acute cardiovascular events, as all three diets had healthy cardioprotective eating patterns, the groups were randomized to a Mediterranean diet, yet with a potent 40, for the risk of cardiovascular complications. Within a 30% reduction was observed. % Reduction within stroke risk. Adherence to the Mediterranean diet was measured in PREDIMED with a hardcore, validated, 14-item screening tool (Mediterranean Diet Adherence Screener, or MADIT score) and found to be inversely related to the rate of heart events. Other analyzes on the PREDIMED study population showed that the Mediterranean diet appeared to reduce the expression of pro-atherogenic genes, cardiovascular risk surrogate markers such as waist-to-hip ratio, lipid fraction, lipoprotein particles, oxidative stress, and Characteristics of markers. Inflammation, but also the risk of developing metabolic syndrome and sort 2 diabetes.

Nevertheless, the initial clues from the PREDIMED study were challenged solely by the three intervention groups due to the low rates of cardiac events that could induce the statistically significant differences considering the incomplete randomization procedure, which Allows for biases within certain gases. Characteristics of basic groups. S chose to withdraw the primary publication and redistribute the information after the exclusion of web sites with randomization deviations; The result still showed significant reductions in the rate of heart events (within the group adhering to a supplement with 31% extra-virgin vegetable oil and within 28% of the group following a supplement with mixed nuts).

Attempts to adapt to the Mediterranean eating style and seek related cardiovascular benefits exist today beyond the boundaries of the Mediterranean. Indian patients with a pre-existing coronary heart condition or high heart risk were included in another randomized trial, a so-called "Indo-Mediterranean diet" that includes whole grains, fruits, vegetables, walnuts, almonds, mustard or soybean oil Is rich in To bring a higher content of omega-3 fatty acids, and compared the random effects group to a Phase I National Cholesterol Education Program (NCEP) diet. Patients who followed the "Indo-Mediterranean Diet" had a reduction in heart rate of approximately 60% and within risk for nonfatal myocardial infarction by about 50%. Adherence to the Mediterranean diet was related to a significantly lower rate of cardiovascular events during a large cohort study that measured 12.2 years of beneficial effects for 23,902 UK participants, as a statistical effect during the study, Significantly inferior treatment in PREDIMED is responsible for imperfection, a transferable ground in the limited transferability of dietary habits. Usage diet contained within the British population. Two studies within the

US have confirmed that significant decreases in the rate of heart events were also observed within the US population at high rates of adherence to the Mediterranean diet.

At the upper levels of the evidence pyramid, a gradual meta-analysis of previous cohort studies also acknowledged the association of the Mediterranean diet with lower rates of cardiac morbidity and mortality. A meta-analysis of randomized controlled trials comparing the effect of a Mediterranean diet versus a low-fat diet on cardiovascular risk factors showed significant benefits overweight, body mass index, vital signs, fasting glycemia, total cholesterol, and high-. Sensitive C-reactive proteins, with no significant differences in LDL (LDL) - cholesterol and HDL (HDL) -cholesterol levels. Another meta-analysis of the latent controlled trial examined the results of Mediterranean-like eating patterns within the primary prevention of the disorder and suggested gains on total and LDL-cholesterol levels.

Separate studies confirmed that adherence to the Mediterranean diet was related to the positive development of abdominal obesity, favorable weight change, and lower incidence of overweight and obesity. The protection provided by the Mediterranean diet against the occurrence of type 2 diabetes was confirmed by a scientific review and meta-analysis considering several dietary patterns. From the studies included during this meta-analysis, two prospective clinical trials, one in healthy volunteers and, therefore, in patients with a history of myocardial infarct, specifically estimated the benefits of the Mediterranean diet within the prevention of type 2 DM. Was designed to apply. Both tests found better adherence to the Mediterranean diet related to a lower risk of developing diabetes. A sub-analysis within the EPIC study described an inverse relationship between adherence to the Mediterranean diet and, therefore, the risk of developing diabetes. Already, the study of patients with type 2 diabetes was scanty, mostly cross-sectional and small-scale, which may explain why some of them prove an advantage of the Mediterranean diet over the criteria that evaluate glycemic control. Were ready, while others were neutral. The result is, however, no fatal effects were identified, and the benefit was confirmed in terms of decreased heart risk in type 2 diabetes patients. Nevertheless, several meta-analyses, including clinical trials in already diagnosed type 2 diabetes patients, also suggest a beneficial effect of the Mediterranean diet on glycemic control, the development of plasma glucose and glycated hemoglobin (HbA1c) levels.

Is evaluated by analyzes focus on potential benefits in other chronic diseases, following studies showing the protective effects of the Mediterranean diet against cardiovascular and metabolic diseases. A primary indication of a possible favorable effect of the Mediterranean diet on cancer morbidity and mortality was seen during a secondary analysis of the Lyon Diet Cardiac Study. The low rate of cancer death was then seen in several studies in the Swedish and American populations. With recent systematic reviews and meta-analyzes, improved adherence to the Mediterranean diet appears to have an inverse relationship with overall cancer mortality and, therefore, colorectal, breast, gastric, liver, head and neck, gallbladder and bile. There is a risk of duct cancer. Another focused review suggests a lower rate for the Mediterranean diet of all digestive cancers other than carcinoma. The EPIC study could be a large-scale prospective study in 10 European countries, including 521,468 adults who followed a period of 15 years for various cancers, cardiovascular, metabolic, neurodegeneration and nutritional outcomes; Research is ongoing in several working groups and current, or future publications are expected to shed light on pathways linking cancer and nutrition. For the immediate, some components of the Mediterranean diet were suggested to have a strong association with benefits within primary and secondary prevention of cancer.

Some data against non-alcoholic liver disease indicate a protective effect of the Mediterranean diet, with better adherence to the low severity of hepatic steatosis and lower levels of alanine — both cross-sectional and in some lower-numbers, Short term prospective study. Finally, the Mediterranean diet may not protect from the occurrence of neurodegenerative diseases. In European and US populations, and improved adherence to the Mediterranean diet was found to be related to lower risk for cognitive decline and the development of Alzheimer's disease. A prospective study on 131,368 participants within a health study of US health professionals and nurses showed that higher adherence scores to the Mediterranean diet were related to a 25% reduction in the risk of developing Parkinson's disease. Consistent with a 2014 systematic review and meta-analysis, an increased response to the Mediterranean diet was related to a 33% lower risk of mild cognitive impairment or Alzheimer's disease and a lower progression from mild cognitive impairment to a greater Alzheimer's disease.

The figures outlined earlier, coming from populations living in India, the UK and therefore us, are not the only attempts to adapt the Mediterranean diet to countries outside the Mediterranean basin. A 12-month longitudinal study on healthy Chilean male workers, in which the Mediterranean diet was applied within the workplace canteen, achieved improvements in waist circumference, HDL-cholesterol, and vital signs values, thus reducing the prevalence of metabolic syndrome by up to 35%. Another 2-year longitudinal study on obese Israeli workers randomly achieved significant weight, triglycerides, and total cholesterol reduction in a calorie-restricted Mediterranean diet; During another 4-year follow-up of the initial subjects, a low-fat diet was significantly more important in whole weight loss than that achieved by a diet or a low-carb diet, thus suggesting these metabolic benefits originate from a Could be better long term adherence.

During a set of studies on firefighting, a profession at high risk for cardio-metabolic disease, the greater weight of the Mediterranean diet, was related to significant improvements in LDL-cholesterol and HDL-cholesterol values, in total weight loss. With body fat cans, and the prevalence of metabolic syndrome and higher popularity scores and better adherence among Fire Service members. These figures can also be justified by the indulgent and attractive lifestyles that characterize the Mediterranean diet, which include neither total interrelationship in any food group, nor calorie count.

Attempts to understand the mechanisms involved within the positive effects of the Mediterranean diet on the risk of cardiometabolic, cognitive or neoplastic diseases cover an increasing number of publications in recent years. Perhaps the simplest thanks to explaining the advantages of the Mediterranean diet is to simultaneously explore it with the simplest examples of the concept of "food synergy", which may be a core element in modern nutrition. Different nutrients and foods present many interactions and mutually enhance their positive effects, in a measure that no different eating principles are often taken apart from the context of the whole dietary pattern or brought about by the Mediterranean diet Used as a separate explanation for the benefits taken. Altogether. In summary, the pathways are often organized as at least one or more of the effects of the Mediterranean diet on various diseases: lipid-lowering and modifying effects; Anti-inflammatory, anti-oxidative, and anti-aggregating effects; Modulation of hormones or growth factors such as cancer-prone mediators; Thanks to changes within the diet's amino alkanoic acid content compared to other eating styles, decreased stimulation of the hormonal or other- and intracellular circulating pathways involved within the development of metabolic diseases and cancer; Changes in the gut microbiota, driving a modified production of bacterial metabolites. A sub-analysis within the PREDIMED trial found that an improved polyphenol intake all correlated with lower mortality; A statistically significant difference was observed for stall ones and lignans, with no significant relationship between flavonoids or phenolic acids and overall mortality. Other data also arise from the PREDIMED trial which indicates advantages induced by consumption of upward amounts of vegetable oil within the diet; An increase of one-ten grams of extra-virgin vegetable oil per day was related to a tenth decrease in the rate of nonfatal heart events and a 7% decrease in the rate of cardiac deaths; The rate of cancer and all-cause deaths were not significantly affected during this report. Vegetable oil should be understood as a vegetable fat that mainly consists of monounsaturated fatty acids, such as monounsaturated fatty acids, but also polyunsaturated fatty acids such as linoleic acids. Since vegetable oil represents the most source of dietary fat (milk, butter, cream, cheese, or meat intake is significantly lower in traditional Mediterranean diets than in other eating patterns), it is used in cooking the entire amount of saturated fat. It allows as little as 8%, sometimes during the entire lifetime of a private. The high content in vegetable oil polyphenols and phytochemicals continues antioxidant actions and reduces the oxidation of unsaturated fatty acids in its composition. Also, the complete antioxidant capacity of the Mediterranean diet is met by the phytochemicals found in whole grains and antioxidant vitamins found in vegetables and fruits. In addition to vegetable oil, a healthy balance of fatty acids within the Mediterranean diet is met by the continued consumption of nuts, seeds, and whole grains, and polyunsaturated fatty acids brought on by moderate or high fish intake. The high content of vegetable fiber brought about by the rich consumption of whole grains, legumes, and fruits reduces insulin resistance, inhibits the absorption of cholesterol within the intestine and cholesterol synthesis within the liver, thus contributing to normal cardiovascular protection. Phytosterols made from nuts, whole grains, seeds, vegetables, and fruits also contribute to controlling intestinal absorption of cholesterol.

A systematic review of experimental studies examining the relationship between the Mediterranean diet and transcriptome activity in different tissues found evidence to support this association, although a comparatively small number of research papers were provided. In addition to the anti-inflammatory functions of monounsaturated fatty acids found in virgin vegetable oil, the peroxyl derivatives found in vegetable oil such as tyrosyl, and lignans also affect cell cycle expression, while oleanolic and malonic acids such as terpenes. The animal model has a modular effect on genes acting on the circadian punch.

The Mediterranean Lifestyle

Mediterranean Diet Nowadays: Between cultural erosion and worldwide recognition, like all opposite regions of the planet, Mediterranean countries were not prepared to reduce the current trend of globalization with all cultures, including those related to food. Worldwide, Bhudia is putting a clear seal on food choices, and the exchange of agricultural products, cuisines, and traditions has become a daily rule. As a Western food culture, technologies and advertising are driven by strong economic power; they tend to exert a marked influence on traditional eating habits and to substitute them in their traditional home as well. All this has been caused by the ever-increasing diseases related to excess weight and food and drink among the last generations of the Mediterranean-neighboring population. Lifestyle standardization, retailing development, low awareness and appreciation for traditional food cultures are left by modern generations, left in favor of the latest, socioeconomically driven changes, the integration of women into the market, thereby limiting culinary activities. Mediterranean food cultures appear to possess a function within erosion. Several surveys of dietary habits conducted in the Mediterranean were within the study of the first seven countries to participate in and characterized by low rates of cardiovascular events (Crete, Greece, Nicotra, Revelator and, Italy) of Mediterranean dietary traditions by increasing the decreasing effect. Reduced intakes of saturated fatty acids, animal foods, cakes, pies, cookies, and sweet drinks, and intakes of monounsaturated fatty acids. Of most concern is the low rate of adherence to the Mediterranean diet in many studies among children and adolescents in Cyprus and Greece.

Currently, environmental difficulties are challenging the sustainability of living Mediterranean life. Water scarcity in most Mediterranean-neighboring countries is driven by both decreased water availability and increased water needs, with agricultural demand currently accounting for 64% of entire water expenditure. Land wastage also has fatal consequences on food production. Reasons for land degradation include expansion of urbanization and associated infrastructure, industrial and solid waste pollution, wind and water degradation, salinization and alkalization, expansion of tourism-prone areas, sand encroachment, degradation of organic matter, all limited possibilities. Agricultural-soil expansion. There is also an echo of global climate change within the Mediterranean basin, as they induce not only water scarcity and land degradation but also the failure of crops, fisheries and livestock productions. Finally, species biodiversity is steadily declining within the Mediterranean (previously the wealthiest in the world) and with a negative impact on local agricultural production, an inclination towards monoculture and standardized farming practices is often seen.

Given the nutritional challenges facing today, the pyramid-form graphical representation of proper Mediterranean eating patterns had to vary to adapt to a world where obesity is driven by a sedentary and hypersaline lifestyle with an epidemic. For example, the Pyramids of the new Mediterranean Diet Foundation Expert Group introduced the concept of "staple food" to emphasize the importance of fertilizer consumption in each of those meals. Austerity and moderation are also advised on the sides of the pyramid. Other diet-related elements such as regular workouts, adequate rest, pleasure, and the importance of conviction and culinary activities seen as positive occupations, leading to high-esteem local habits, biodiversity, seasonal and therefore traditional, local use. Necessary. And environmentally friendly food products are also highlighted. Research is additionally aimed at evaluating the combined benefits achieved by combining Mediterranean eating patterns with systematic induction of weight loss. An external randomized clinical trial, PREDIMED-PLUS, performed by an equivalent team of Spanish investigators as PREDIMED and combined with a three-point weight-intervention using a similar type of Mediterranean-style dietary intervention, Randomization of 6874 participants ended in December 2016, with restrictions on energy intake, physical activity, recommendations, and behavior modification. And was predicted to close in March 2022; The design of the study, some foundational, and cross-sectional analysis in PREDIMED-PLUS have recently been published.

Struggling for stability and economic survival in their homes, the Mediterranean diet must also overcome obstacles in other regions of the planet, where its health benefits are recognized by the medical profession, but adoption by communities dominated by less healthy Westerners Limited thanks for the behavior. Countries in Northern Europe have started adopting the way the Mediterranean eats, thanks to the increasing availability of Mediterranean fruits and vegetables in local stores and well-run public health policies. The acquisition is restricted within the US, although modern nutritional guidelines have incorporated Mediterranean eating patterns into their appropriately healthy dietary patterns. Paradoxically enough, the Mediterranean diet is no longer considered a diet for the socially helpless classes, as it was immediately Ansel Keys made his first scientific observations, but a diet for people with a better socioeconomic status. However, the reality beneath this idea is not absolute. A better education level is more geared towards people learning about healthy foods, keeping in mind the dietary health advice coming from local and international cities and ultimately providing a better variability and diversity to their food choices Huh. However, when money spending is strictly talked about, Mediterranean diet prices are on the verge of a Westernized diet, as supplemental spending on fruits and vegetables is less than that spent on meat, sweets, sweets, and fast food. Occur. A prudent approach to applying Mediterranean eating habits to populations living elsewhere compared to Mediterranean coasts may be to look first for local dietary habits after taking an adapted nutrition survey, then these newly identified foods to spot, to match the pattern of the first Mediterranean diet. To adapt local habits for healthy Mediterranean people in some key points, without completely giving up on the main differences and exact character of local food cultures.

Chapter 2: Advantages of the Mediterranean Diet and The Main Benefits of Using an Air Fryer

It Is Good for Your Heart

"This is probably the most important known benefit," Moore says. "Mediterranean diet has been shown to reduce the risk of heart condition, stroke, and early death, all related to improved heart health." This is because this diet is high in heart-healthy omega-3s as an antioxidant from c-food, nuts, and vegetable oils, as well as all those fruits and vegetables.

It Enhances Brain Health

All those healthy fats are also good for your brain. A study with 1,864 participants found that those following a Mediterranean diet were less likely to experience Alzheimer's urge or experience other types of cognitive decline in adulthood. There is an immediate correlation between fish consumption and the low risk of Alzheimer's.

It Can Help with Depression and Anxiety

Due to psychiatrist and Well + Good Wellness counselor Drew Ramsey, MD is a vegetable and healthy fat-rich diet that makes it a part of their treatment for patients with depression, anxiety, or other psychiatric conditions: bananas, spinach, and eggs are great in your gut. Bacteria have been shown to spice up, and serially, your mood. One study found that when older adults followed the Mediterranean diet, they were less likely to experience depression.

This Can Help Stabilize Blood Sugar

Unlike other popular eating plans, the Mediterranean diet is big on whole grains and other healthy carbs - and comes with huge benefits. Says Beckman, "Complex whole-grain carbohydrates instead of refined grains, such as buckwheat, wheat berries, and quinoa, help maintain your blood sugar levels as well as help with all your energy. "

It Is Associated with Reducing the Risk of Cancer

When researchers examined a combined 27 studies - considering more than 2 million people - they found that the Med diet is that eating plans are associated with a lower risk of cancer ethics, particularly carcinoma, carcinoma, and gastric cancer.

It Promotes Healthy Weight Management

"Because of all the fiber, the Mediterranean diet is useful in managing fullness," Moore says. "You feel more satiated with foods high in fiber, which helps in healthy weight loss and metabolism." The key: replacing simple carbohydrates with fibrous fruits, vegetables, legumes, and beans.

It Has Special Benefits for Post-Menopausal Women

Mediterranean diet has also been linked to the positive effects of bone and muscle in post-menopausal women. This was little study, so more research is needed, but it is promising because previous studies have found that menopause can reduce the bone and muscle of women.

It Is Good for Your Stomach

One study has found that people who follow a Mediterranean diet have a better population of excellent bacteria in their microbiome than those who eat a standard Western diet. Researchers noted an increase in eating plant-based foods such as vegetables, fruits, and legumes, which put the great bacteria above 7 percent - not too shabby.

It Is Associated with Prolonged Stay

As if all the above benefits are not enough, it is also associated with living an extended life- mainly due to the above-mentioned better heart health. There is a reason why many of these "blue areas" are within the Mediterranean!

There is no single definition of a Mediterranean diet, but a group of scientists used the post-2015 basis of research.

Vegetables: Include 3 to 9 servings each day.

Fresh Fruit: Up to 2 servings each day.

Cereals: Most whole grains from 1 to 13 servings each day.

Oil: Up to eight servings of extra cold vegetable oil each day.

Fat - mostly unsaturated - makes up 37% of the entire calories. Unsaturated fat comes from plant sources, such as olives and avocados. The Mediterranean diet also provides 33 grams (g) of fiber each day.

The baseline diet for this study provides approximately 2,200 calories each day.

Main Ingredients of the Mediterranean Diet and their Benefits

Here are some sample ingredients that often include people within the Mediterranean diet.

Vegetables: tomatoes, peppers, onions, eggplants, zucchini, cucumber, leafy green vegetables, and others.

Fruits: Watermelon, apple, apricot, peach, orange, and lemon, and so on.

Beans: Beans, lentils, and chickpeas.

Nuts and seeds: almonds, walnuts, sunflower seeds, and cashews.

Unsaturated fats: vegetable oil, sunflower seed oil, olives, and avocado.

Dairy products: Cheese and yogurt are the most used dairy foods.

Grains: These are mostly whole grains and include wheat and rice along with bread along with many meals.

Fish: sardines and other oily fish, also in the form of oyster and other shellfish.

Poultry: Chicken or turkey.

Eggs: Chicken, quail and duck eggs.

Drinks: A person can drink alcohol carefully.

The Mediterranean diet does not include strong alcohol or carbonated and sweetened beverages. According to one definition, the diet limits meat and sweets, but 2 servings per week.

Healthy fats: Diets are low in saturated fat and high in monounsaturated fat. Health experts recommend limiting the intake of saturated fat to avoid high cholesterol, obesity, and disorder.

Fiber: A diet that consists of whole grains and legumes, as well as fresh fruits and vegetables, is high in fiber. Fiber promotes healthy digestion and reduces the risk of bowel cancer and disorder. It is also going to reduce the risk of type 2 diabetes.

Vitamins and minerals: Fruits and vegetables provide vitamins and minerals, which are essential for the healthy functioning of the body. Also, lean meat provides vitamin B-12, which is rare in a completely plant-based diet.

Antioxidant: Antioxidants include vitamins, minerals, and other molecules that will help remove free radicals from the body. Free radicals are toxic molecules that will form as a byproduct of metabolism and other processes. They will cause damage that will cause cancer and other diseases. Dietary antioxidants help protect the body by removing free radicals, and plant foods are good sources of antioxidants.

Low sugar: Fresh fruits provide natural sugar, but diets are low in added sugar. Added sugar is high in calories and increases the risk of obesity and its complications. The American Heart Association (AHA) recommends limiting the intake of added sugar to six teaspoons per day for women and 9 teaspoons per day for men. This is equal to 24 grams and 36 grams, respectively. Instead of sugar sweets, people will eat fruits on a Mediterranean diet.

The Mediterranean Diet Can Help Reduce Your Risk for Heart Conditions: Several studies show that the Mediterranean diet is sweet for your ticker, a meta-analysis published in November 2015 by the Journal for Review in Food Science and Nutrition.

A randomized clinical trial published in April 2013 within the New England Journal of Drugs in April 2013 provided perhaps the most convincing evidence. For nearly five years, Spain followed 7,000 women and men who had a high risk of type 2 diabetes or the disorder. Those who ate a calorie-unrestricted Mediterranean diet with extra-virgin vegetable oil or nuts had a 30 percent lower risk of cardiovascular events. The researchers did not recommend exercise to the participants.

The study reassessed information at a later point to deal with flaws widely criticized within the Randomization Protocol, and a similar report by June 2018 within the New England Journal of Drugs.

Eating the Mediterranean Diet can reduce women's risk of stroke.

We have already known that eating during the Mediterranean fashion may reduce the risk of eating disorders in some people. Well, the diet may also help reduce the risk of stroke in women, although researchers did not follow an equivalent lead for men, which is consistent with a cohort study published within the journal Stroke in September 2018.

Researchers examined a predominantly white group of 23,232 men and women aged between 40 and 77 living in the UK. The more closely a woman followed a Mediterranean diet, the lower her risk of stroke. However, the researchers did not see statistically significant clues for males. Most notably, in women who had a higher risk of stroke, following a diet reduced the likelihood of this health event by 20 percent.

Studies do not know the rationale for the difference, but they hypothesize that different types of stroke may play a role in men and women. Carson says an honest next step would be a clinical trial to understand the explanation behind the differences.

A Mediterranean diet can prevent cognitive decline and Alzheimer's disease. As a heart-healthy diet, Mediterranean eating patterns can also help reduce your memory and thinking skills decline with age. "The brain can be a very hungry organ. To provide all these nutrients and oxygen [that it needs], you've got an upscale blood supply. Therefore, people who are having a problem with their vascular health - their blood vessels - actually have an increased risk for developing problems with their brain so that it would be in the form of regular cognitive decline, "Keith Fargo, Ph.D., Director of Scientific Programs and Says. Outreach to the Alzheimer's Association.

What's more, funded by the National Institute on Aging. A small study published within the journal Neurology in E2018 examined brain scans for 70 people who initially had no signs of dementia and scored them in a way close to their food. The Mediterranean pattern Those who participated less often had beta-amyloid deposits (brain-related Alzheimer's disease-related protein plaques) at the top of the study and less energy within the brain. At least two years later, these individuals also showed a greater reduction in deposits and energy use - potentially indicating a greater risk for Alzheimer's - than they did. Who followed the Mediterranean diet more closely?

Advantages and Disadvantages of the Mediterranean Diet

Pros:

General

Nutrition Medium diet encourages the elimination of any food groups and the proliferation of nutrient-dense foods, making it easier to meet their nutritional needs.

Heart Health

scientists have conducted a strong amount of research on the Mediterranean diet and cardiovascular health, both also in the form of controlled trials in observational studies. A review study within the European Journal of Clinical Nutrition concluded that adherence to the Mediterranean diet is related to a lower risk of coronary heart condition, attack, and overall mortality.

Improved Blood Sugar Control

A systematic review found that the Mediterranean diet was poised to reduce hemoglobin A1C levels by 0.47 percent compared to the control diet. In the last three months, hemoglobin A1C shows blood sugar control in your body. Although it seems small, any deficiency can be helpful for people with diabetes who try to manage blood sugar levels.

Mental Health

A surprising benefit may be the relationship between the Mediterranean diet and improved psychological state, consistent with Kelly Toups, MLA, RD, LDN, Director of Nutrition for Old ways.

"A 2018 study in molecular psychiatry found that those most closely adhering to the Mediterranean diet were 33% less likely to develop incident depression than those not following the Mediterranean diet."

Also, consider the stress on social relations within the Mediterranean lifestyle. It is often paramount for the psychological state, especially in older adults. Loneliness can be reduced by maintaining friendship and regular social contact, which is considered positive for overall health.

Weight Management

It seems counter-intuitive that a diet that emphasizes calorie-dense vegetable oils and nuts can help with weight management. However, these saturated fats — recommended in conjunction with various fiber-rich vegetables and fruits — can help you feel fuller.

Reduces Inflammatory Markers

Inflammation can be a hot topic recently, as doctors and researchers establish a relationship between certain inflammatory markers and chronic disease. For example, two high-level inflammatory markers (interleukin 6 and C reactive protein) are thought to be related to an increased risk of diabetes. Research suggests that the Mediterranean diet is related to lower levels of those inflammatory markers.

Cancer Prevention

Most cases of cancer are not caused by a singular factor, but by a mixture of several genetic and environmental factors. Diet may play a role during this complex disease, and some dietary patterns — including the Mediterranean diet — are related to lower risk of cancer.

For example, a meta-analysis found that those who followed the Mediterranean diet most closely included colorectal cancer, carcinoma, gastric cancer, liver cancer of the liver, head and neck cancer, and the development of prostatic adenocarcinoma. There was a risk.

Cons:

There are only a few cons to the Mediterranean diet, as it is quite balanced and well researched. However, there can also be a couple of challenges to beat.

Price

Although branded foods or special supplements are not, some consumers regularly worry about the value of including fish. Seafood tends to be costlier than other proteins. However, there are many ways to buy on a budget - even for seafood.

Additional Guidance may also Be Necessary for Diabetics

although studies suggest that a Mediterranean diet may reduce diabetes risk and better control blood sugar - some people with diabetes may have additional guidance on this diet. Because there is stress on grains, fruits, and vegetables (including starchy vegetables), food can also be high in carbohydrates. People with diabetes need to consume an equal, controlled amount of carbohydrate throughout the day to avoid blood-sugar glucose.

High-fiber Diets May Help Control Diabetes

The Mediterranean diet is high in fiber-rich foods, which are said to aid in regulating blood sugar by absorbing blood sugar.

This, in turn, can help prevent and manage type 2 diabetes, the common type of diabetes.

The Mediterranean diet encourages consumption of nutrient-dense foods and the top ingredient

Dynan explained that the Mediterranean diet promotes consumption of whole plant-based foods such as vegetables, fresh fruits, whole grains, legumes, and nuts. They stated that these foods guarantee a high intake of important minerals, vitamins, and phytonutrients, suggesting a supply of beneficial effects on metabolic and inflammatory risk parameters.

Dynan also told insider that the Mediterranean diet concentrates on whole foods and eliminates low-quality, highly processed foods that are often full of additives, sugar, and unhealthy fats.

This diet plan allows you to interrupt and luxuriate food

"Diet on said that the Mediterranean diet is not just about food." The Mediterranean diet, she explained, advocates for us to interrupt, enjoy food and engage with our food and, therefore, the people with whom we taste it.

However, the diet has no calorie guidelines

"because there's no limit, it's often difficult to not have a selected plan or calorie guidelines". Also, since the focus is on healthy fats and whole grains, he explained that overwriting is possible. Additionally, she said that this diet promotes eating whole foods, like full-fat dairy products, which, if eaten in large amounts, can be very dense.

Benefits of Combining an Air Fryer with a Low Carb Diet

Here are some ways an air fryer complements a low carb diet:

- You can enjoy fried foods without carbs.
- It makes cooking reception fast and easy.
- Versatile cooking keeps things interesting.

Enjoy Fried Foods on a low carb diet. Fried foods are very unhealthy and a natural part of any diet. But air fryers turn to that. Their revolutionary cooking method allows you to realize crispy, fried foods without added oil. It makes it possible to enjoy fried foods by sticking with a diet.

Opt for a low carb option when frying foods for the keto diet. Walnut flour is an excellent alternative to low carb breakers. For a touch, extra texture, try finely chopped nuts instead of employing nut flour. Spray or toss foods with a saturated or monounsaturated cooking fat such as avocado oil, copra oil, or macadamia oil.

Chapter 3: Example of A Balanced Meal Plan and Useful Tips That Will Help You Every Day

Below you can find some weekly sample menus of the Mediterranean diet.

Feel free to regulate portions and food choices that support your own needs and preferences.

Example n.1

Monday

Breakfast:

Greek yogurt with strawberries and oats.

Lunch:

Whole grain sandwiches with vegetables.

Dinner:

A tuna fish salad dressed in vegetable oil. A little fruit for dessert.

Tuesday

Breakfast:

Oatmeal with Raisins.

Lunch:

Leftover tuna fish salad before night.

Dinner:

Salad with tomatoes, olives, and feta cheese.

Wednesday

Breakfast:

Omelet with vegetable, tomato, and onion. Some fruit.

Lunch:

Whole grain sandwiches with cheese and fresh vegetables.

Dinner:

Mediterranean Lasagna.

Thursday

Breakfast:

Yogurt with sliced fruits and nuts.

Lunch:

Leftover laze from the night before.

Dinner:

Served with brewed salmon, rice and vegetables.

Friday

Breakfast:

Eggs and vegetables, fried in vegetable oil.

Lunch:

Greek yogurt with strawberries, oats, and nuts.

Dinner: Grilled lamb, salad and potatoes.

Saturday

Breakfast:

Oatmeal with raisins, nuts and an apple.

Lunch:

Whole grain sandwiches with vegetables.

Dinner:

Mediterranean pizza made with whole wheat, topped with cheese, vegetables, and olives.

Sunday

Breakfast:

Omelet with vegetables and olives.

Lunch:

Leftover pizza before night.

Dinner:

Grilled chicken, with vegetables and a potato. Fruit for dessert.

Example n.2

Day 1

Breakfast:

A pan-fried egg

Whole-wheat toast for grilled tomatoes

For extra calories add another egg or some chopped avocado

Lunch:

Mixed with cherry tomatoes and olives on top Salad greens 2 cups and a dressing of wholegrain oil and vinegar.

Whole-grain pita bread

2 ounces of hummus (oz)

Dinner:

Spaghetti sauce, grilled vegetables and low-fat whole-grain pizzas topping for added cheese

For extra calories add some chopped chicken, ham, tuna or pine nuts to the pizza

Day 2

Breakfast:

1 cup Greek yogurt

Half a cup of fruit, such as blueberries, raspberries, or sliced nectar

For extra calories add 1-2 ounces of almonds or walnuts

Lunch:

Grilled vegetables, eggplant, zucchini, capsicum, onion, and the like whole grain

For extra calories add stuffing to increase calories: you can use hummus or avocado smeared on the bread

Dinner:

A portion of baked cod with garlic and black pepper

Add to taste a roasted potato along with vegetable oil and chives.

Day 3

Breakfast:

1 cup of whole-grain oats with date

Fruits with less sugar, such as raspberries

1 oz of chopped almonds (optional)

Lunch:

Boiled white beans with spices, such as laurel, garlic, and cumin

1 cup arugula One With a vegetable oil dressing and toppings of tomato, cucumber, and feta cheese

Dinner:

Half Cup Grain Pasta with Spaghetti Sauce, Olive Oil, and Grilled Vegetables

Parmesan Cheesecake 1 tbsp

Day 4

Breakfast:

Capsicum, onion, tomato and two eggs clash with 1 oz of top queso fresco or a quarter of an avocado

Lunch:

Anchovies with a sprinkling of juice on whole-grain toast in roasted vegetable oil

A warm salad consisting of 2 cups of boiled bananas and tomatoes

Dinner:

2 teaspoons of boiled spinach juice and herbs, vegetable oil with boiled artisan with garlic powder and salt

For extra calories add another artichoke to get a hearty meal

Day 5

Breakfast:

1 cup of Greek yogurt with Cinnamon and Shishir honey, sliced apples and chopped almonds

Lunch:

Bell pepper, dried tomatoes with 1 cup quinoa olive sun

Garbanzo beans wishful of Areaway leaf parsley, roast the feta cheese

Crumbles Sathish avocado (optional)

Dinner:

2 cups steamed black tomato, cucumber, olives, juice, parmesan cheese and a piece of grilled sardines with lemon slices

Day 6

Breakfast:

Two slices of whole-grain toast with soft cheese. queso fresco, or chevre

Chopped blueberries or figs

Lunch:

Greens mixed with tomatoes, 2 cups of cucumber vegetable oil and a small portion of roasted chicken with a sprinkling of juices

Dinner:

Oven-Roasted Vegetables, such as:

- Artichoke
- Carrot
- Zucchini
- Eggplant
- Sweet Potato
- Tomatoes

Day 7

Breakfast:

Cinnamon grains, seeds and whole grains with palm trees, and low-sugar fruits, such as raspberry or blackberry.

Lunch:

Stuffed Zucchini, Yellow Squash, Onion, and Tomato and Herb Sauce

Dinner:

2 cups of greens, such as arugula or spinach, tomatoes, olives, and a small portion of white fish with the leftover vegetable stew of lunch with vegetable oil.

Chapter 4: Air Fried Mediterranean Breakfast Recipes

Air Fryer Sushi Roll

Ingredients

For Salad Cal:

- 1 1/2 cups chopped - remove ribs
- 1/2 teaspoon rice vinegar
- 3/4 teaspoon toasted vegetable oil
- 1/8 teaspoon garlic powder

- 1/4 teaspoon ground ginger
- 3/4 teaspoon Soy
- 1 tablespoon sesame seeds - toasted or not - your phone!

for Kale Salad Sushi Roll:

- 1 Batch Autoclave Sushi Rice Chilled to
- Sushi Nori
- Hass Avocado 1/2- Sliced used
- Temperature Mayo Banas Vezina
- Make for the coating to 1/2 cup panko breadcrumbs

Instructions

- Kale salad combines, in a large bowl, vinegar, vegetable oil, garlic powder, ginger, and soy. With clean hands, massage the bud until it turns bright green. Stir within sesame seeds and set aside.
- Make black salad sushi rolls Spread Of naughty
- A sheet on a dry surface. With slightly moist fingers, grab a pair of rice and spread it on the nori. It is thought that the thin layer of rice must be covered with almost the entire sheet. With an edge, you want the naked seaweed to move about 1/2 "away. Consider this because the flap that will take off your roll.
- Unlike that naked part on top of the seaweed, about 2-3. Lie. Top with tablespoons of kale salad and a few slices of

avocado. Start at the top with the filling, roll your sushi, press gently to insist on a pleasant, tight roll. Once you at the top. Use that naked little one. Seaweed to seal off the rolls. If necessary, wet your fingers, and let it Wet a little seaweed to

- Repeat 2-3 steps to roll more than 3 sushi rolls.
- Make casserole taco mayo in raita
- Mix the shallow bowl. Fast the mayo with the, until you reach that warm level. Add more 1/2 teaspoon at a time until you find the spicy mayo.
- Fry slices
- Grab your first sushi roll, and coat it as evenly as possible within Sri Krishna, then within Panko. Put the roll in your air fryer basket. Repeat with the remainder of your sushi roll.
- Air fry at 390F for 10 minutes, shaking gently after 5 minutes.
- When the roll is cooled enough to handle, grab an upright knife and gently cut the roll into 6-8 pieces. When you are slicing, consider the saw gently, and do not press it hard with your knife. Which will only send bananas and avocados flying through the ends of your roll?
- Serve soy with a needle

Thai Style Vegetarian Crab

Ingredients

- 400 g / 4 cup Dieted or about 4 medium potatoes
- 1 bunch green onion
- 1 lime, zest, and juice
- 1½ inch fresh ginger
- 1 tbsp tamari, or soy

- 4 tbsp Thai red curry paste
- 1 x 398 g palm hearts, drained, long tubular shaped ones work best. (Dry weight at approx. 200g)
- 100g / can cup canned artichoke hearts, dried
- black pepper, to salt to taste
- 2 tablespoons oil for frying the pan, peel the optional

Instructions

- Cube the potatoes and then pan them. Add to Cover with water and boil until the boils are tender and mashable but not too soft, then drain, mash and keep aside.
- While the potatoes are boiling, add green onion, juice, lime zest, ginger, tamarind, and curry paste to a kitchen appliance. Break the nori sheets into manageable pieces and insert them within the kitchen appliance with contrasting material. Process until there is a paste. Nori remains a touch chunkier than everything else, which is fine.
- Dry the palm hearts well, and either grates them or mix them with a fork, then cut the artichokes and coarsely. Be sure to empty them thoroughly and provide a touch squeeze to the artichokes to insist any residual liquid in them.
- Once the potato has cooled down enough to handle, add the pasta and shake well so that it is evenly distributed

then add the sliced heart of the palm and so the sliced artichoke and shake gently.

- Form in the patties and place them on a tray with some baking parchment as they go. You will either pan-fry them, bake the oven or cook them on a grate to cook. They are the best pan-fried as they develop a brilliant golden crust.
- To pan-fry,
- heat a few tablespoons of oil during a pan over medium-high heat. Once hot, add crab cake carefully. Leave them well alone for about 4 minutes to allow a thick, golden layer to develop, then flip over and equalize in the opposite direction. Remove from the pan and put them on some kitchen paper to absorb excess oil. Your pan may not be large enough to cook all of them directly, so keep the oven on low and cook the cooked ones to stay warm.
- Let's
- heat your puzzle for medium-high heat. When hot, carefully place the crab cakes on the grill and cook from all sides for 4-5 minutes.
- To bake the oven, place it
- lightly on a baking parchment tray and bake at 400 ° F for about 25 minutes. Turn halfway.

Bite-Sized Blooming Onion

Ingredients

- 2 pounds cipollini onion, peeled and sectioned
- 2 large eggs
- 1 cup buttermilk
- 2 cups all-purpose flour
- 1 tbsp paprika
- 1 tbsp kosher salt
- 1 tbsp pepper
- 1 tsp garlic powder
- 1 tsp red chili
- vegetable oil, for frying

- 1/4 cup mayo
- 1/4 cup sour cream
- 1 tablespoon ketchup
- 1/2 teaspoon peripheral chic spoonful of salt

Instructions

- The first part often ensures that You can buy the appropriate onions! You cannot use frozen onions or pearl onions. They are a touch too small. You will like these cipollini onions. You will usually find them by the pound in most supermarkets near onions!
- Generally, once you make an outer-blossom onion, you will want to leave the base for the whole thing to stick together. I was born here because I wanted the onions to stick together, but it should be ready to eat in one bite as well and there is no need to worry about the base. I decided to isolate Aadhaar and see how it goes.
- Looks like you'll do it! Trim just enough to spruce up the dirty root but keep the maximum volume intact. Instead, keep the tip end intact! Then peel the onion with just a sharp paper; otherwise, you lick your fingers.
- Next, slice through onions to form squares (such as within the full-size version). If you don't get what you want for the base section, the tip section will hold the onion together. It won't work with a full-sized onion but works fine with

smaller ones. Just take care not to cut it all the way. A spiked knife helps!

- The Real Thing: This is often a very annoying presentation. I did a few tunes, though and worked through two pounds of onions in about a quarter of an hour. As soon as you hang it, they are going fast.

Hum Seth Portobello Mushrooms

Ingredients

- Vinegar
- Salt and pepper
- 4 tablespoons free spaghetti sauce (such as 365 organics)
- 1 clove garlic,
- Oil 3 minutes zucchini, sliced, chopped, or Julienned (about 1/2 medium))
- 2 tablespoons sweet,
- 4 flour kalamata olives,
- 1 teaspoon of dried basil
- Pepper minced 1/2 cup (see note for kalamata version),

- Minced fresh basil leaves or other herbs or happened, then minced

Instructions

- Wash the portobellos thoroughly. Stop the stems and remove the gills with a spoon. Dry and brush the pats or spray each side with balsamic vinegar. Sprinkle inside with salt and pepper.

- Spread 1 tbsp of spaghetti sauce inside each mushroom and sprinkle with garlic.

Air Fryer Instructions:

- Preheat the 330F to the air fryer. Use a rack to move a slot or two layers to as many mushrooms as possible. (You may have to try doing this in batches counting on dimensions or your air fryer and portobellos.) Air fry for 3 minutes.
- Remove the mushrooms and all with equal portions of zucchini, peppers, and olives and sprinkle with dried basil and salt and pepper. Return to the air fryer for 3 minutes. Check mushrooms and employ a rack if. Return to the air fryer for an additional 3 minutes or until the mushrooms are tender. Place on a plate, drizzle with hummus and

sprinkle with basil or other herbs. If you wish, you will put the Port Propeller in the air again to heat the Humor.

- Preheat oven instructions 400F.

- Place the fried portobellos during a baking dish and bake for five minutes. Remove from the oven and sprinkle all with equal portions of zucchini, peppers, and olives, and with dried basil and salt and pepper. Return to the oven and cook until the mushrooms are tender. Place on a plate, drizzle with hummus and sprinkle with basil or other herbs. If you wish, you will warm the humus by briefly putting the portobellos under the broiler.

Notes:

Kalamata is straightforward to make hummus and makes a delicious topping for these individual pizzas. Simply make a batch of hummus within the blender, remove half of it to use normally, and add 8–10 kalamata olives to the remaining humus within the blender. Blend well.

Vegan Air Fryer Eggplant Parmesan

Ingredients

- 1 Large Eggplant Stems and Sliced
- 1/2 C Flour
- 1/2 C Almond Milk
- 1/2 C Panko Breadcrumbs

- 2 Tablespoon Grated Parmesan
- Onion Powder to Powder taste
- Salt and pepper to taste to top the parmesan: or Parmesan for Serving
- to serve more1 c Marinara Sauce
- 1/2 c Vegan Mozzarella Shreds
- Vegan Grated
- 4 oz. Spaghetti or pasta of your choice cooked hard (about 2 ounces. Per person)
- Vegetarian Grated Parmesan Sprinkle
- Garnish for celery

Instructions

- Wash, dry and take away eggplant stems. Make slices.
- Dip the slices in the flour, then the almond milk and finally, the panko bread pieces you just mix with the vegan par man, salt, pepper, garlic, and onion powder.
- Spray lightly with oil (if desired) and place in an air fryer basket at 390 degrees for quarter-hour, flipping halfway (spray lightly on the other side).
- Alternatively, you will do this by beating the oven at 400 degrees. The cooking time can vary as the convection type of the air fryer uses the cooking method. Just keep an eye on them.

- While the eggplant is cooking, stir further and cook your pasta.
- When golden on each side, spoon several marinas and top with a mixture of 2 vegan cheese. Cook until the cheese begins to melt.
- Serve with pasta (and extra sauce), garnishing with fresh parsley and perhaps another sprinkle of vegetarian parmesan. Enjoy it!

Crispy Baked Artichoke Fries

Ingredients

- 1 cup all-purpose flour
- 1/2 - 1 cup vegetable-based milk (I used almonds)
- 1/2 teaspoon garlic powder
- 3/4 teaspoon salt

- 1/4 tsp black pepper, to taste for a mixer dry
- 1 1/2 cups pancake breadcrumbs
- 1/2 tsp paprika
- 1/4 tsp salt

Instructions

- If you are using an oven, put it at 500F Preheat. Then, remove the can of artichoke hurts and cut them into quarters.
- Place quarter artichoke hearts on one half and clean tea towel during a row. Fold the opposite half towel over the top of the quarter and press gently to get rid of the moisture. When you are preparing the wet and dry mix, allow the artichoke to sit inside the towel.
- Prepare the weight mix by putting all the ingredients in a small bowl with a wide rim. I suggest starting with 1/2 cup of plant milk and behaving your high in 1 tbsp increase. You will want the combination to be slightly thicker than the batter.
- Prepare a dry mix during a small bowl with a wide rim.
- Using different hands for each mix, dip each artichoke quarter into the weight mix, gently shake the surplus batter, then pour it into the dry mix and coat well. Repeat with all artichoke pieces.
- To bake artichoke fries

- In the oven: Place on a greased or lined baking sheet and bake at 500F for 10-13 minutes
- In an air fryer: Bake at 340 F for 10-13 minutes. I baked my fries in 2 batches, so there was some "breathing room" between the fries and they did not stick together.
- Serve hot and with any dipping sauce of your choice.

Note:

You can use any flour for a weighted mix, but every flour absorbs a specific amount of liquid. I can suggest starting with 1/2 cup of plant milk and treat your high in 1 tbsp increments. You will want the combination to be slightly thicker than the batter.

Some Panko Breadcrumbs are not vegetarian, so double-check the ingredients before you buy! I used some from Whole Foods, which were also free of oil.

This recipe is often made gluten-free with GF flour and breadcrumbs!

Vegetarian Corn Fritters

Ingredients

- Fresh Frozen or Grilled Whole Corn Kernels About 2Finely Grilled
- Corn + 2-3 Karachi Almond Milk Plus Salt "For Creamed Corn Blend" / 1 cc of Pepper, for Taste
- 1/3 Cornmeal

- 1/3 c flour
- 1/2 teaspoon yeast
- onion Powder Wad
- garlic powder Shake
- 1/4 teaspoon paprika
- Rake with 2 table green peppers
- about 1/4 c chopped Italian parsley
- Live Nest frying Oil
- The tangy dipping sauce: to
- 4 tbsp vegetarian mayonnaise
- 2 grainy mustard spoon or Swaddle

Instructions

- Dry ingredients (flour with whisk cornmeal, leaven, seasonings, and parsley).
- In a kitchen appliance, 1 tablespoon of corn with 2-3 tablespoons of almond milk. Season with salt and pepper.
- Add corn mixture to flour mixture until well mixed.
- Add two seas of whole corn kernels, folded to the mixture. Do not finish the work and do not add more flour or cornmeal. It will seem loose but will be arranged as soon as they cook.
- Heat a pan on medium-high heat then add about 1 tbsp of oil.

- Using a cookie scoop, firmly place the batter in the pan. Employing a spatula, it quickly flattens to form a patty shape.
- Allow to cook until one side is golden and flip the opposite side to cook.
- Remove paper to get rid of any excess oil. Season with salt.
- Stir the ingredients of the dipping sauce together and serve immediately.

Vegan Bacon-Wrapped Mini Breakfast Burritos

Ingredients

- 2 tablespoons cashew butter
- 2 - 3 tablespoons Tamari
- 1 - 2 tablespoons of liquid smoke
- 1-2 tablespoons water tablespoons
- 4 paper
- 4 serving swages as scrambled or tofu scrambled veggies
- 1/3 cup roasted.
- 8 strips roasted red chili

- 1 small tree broccoli,
- 6-8 stalks fresh asparagus
- handful spinach, kale, other greens

Instructions

- Preheat the oven to 350 ° F. Line the baking sheet with parchment paper.
- In a small shallow bowl, mix cashew butter, tamari, liquid smoke, and water.
- Prepare all the filler to assemble the rolls.
- Rice Paper Hydrating Technique: Able to fill/roll an outer plate/surface. Hold a paper under cold water running from the tap water, wetting each side of the wrapper, for only a few seconds. Remove from the water and while still firm, place it on a plate to fill - the paper will soften as it sits, but will not be so soft that it sticks to the surface or is handled.
- Fill with paper, leaving only the sides, keeping the contents away from the center. Fold two sides like a burrito, roll from component side to another side, and seal. Dip each roll in cashews - liquid smoke mixture, coating completely. Arrange the rolls on a parchment baking sheet.
- Bake at 350 ° F for a quarter of an hour. Remove from the oven, turn, return and continue baking for an additional 10 minutes until the bacon is crispy. Serve hot

Meatless Monday Air Fryer Thai Veggie Bites

Ingredients

- 1 large broccoli
- 1 large cauliflower
- 6 large carrot
- handful of peas
- cauliflower made in rice "
- large onions peeled and dried
- 1 small powder
- 2 leeks cleaned and finely chopped shrimp
- 1 coconut Can be taken in milk.

- 50 gems to 1 cm cube ginger peeled and grated
- 1 tablespoon garlic puree
- 1 tablespoon vegetable oil
- 1 tbsp Thai green curry paste
- 1 tablespoon coriander
- 1 tablespoon
- mix 1 teaspoon cumin
- salt and pepper
- Metric - Imperial

Instructions

- Garlic in a pan, Cook your onion with ginger and onion. Vegetable oil until the onion has a nice bit of color.
- While you are cooking your onions, cook your vegetables (other than the courtyard and the leek) for 20 minutes or until almost cooked.
- Add the agate, leeks and hence curry paste to your pan and cook for 5 minutes on medium heat.
- Add coconut milk and so mix the remaining portion of the spice mixture well, then add cabbage rice.
- Mix again and let simmer for 10 minutes.
- Once it boils for 10 minutes and so the sauce has reduced by half, add boiled vegetables. Mix well and you will now have a surprise base for your veggie bytes.
- Keep in the refrigerator for an hour to chill.

- Make bite-sized pieces and place them in the air fryer after one hour. Cook for 10 minutes at 180c then serves as it cools.

Notes:

For the best results, cover your hands in flour and as you cut the veggies, they are going to take in the flour and make a better combination. Also, keep the cutting on the baking sheet in your air fryer to make it worse later.

Classic Falafel

Ingredients

- 1 ½ cup dry garbanzo beans
- ½ cup chopped fresh parsley
- ½ cup chopped fresh coriander
- ½ cup chopped white onion
- 7 cloves garlic
- 2 Karachi. All-purpose flour

- Small spoon. Sea salt
- 1 tbsp. ground cumin
- . Small spoon. Ground cardamom
- 1 tsp. Ground
- coriander. Small spoon. Red chili

Instructions

- Soak them overnight: Place dried garbanzo beans during the canopy with a large bowl and 1 inch of water. Let sit for 20-24 hours. Drain well. Quick soak: Rinse garbanzo beans during a sieve and raises an outer pot. Cover with 2 inches of water and bring to a boil. Allow boiling for 1 minute, cover the pot and take it away from heat. Represent 1 hour. Drain well.

- In a kitchen appliance bowl, add parsley, cilantro, onion, and garlic. Stir until well mixed.

- Add soaked garbanzo beans, flour, salt, cumin, cardamom, coriander and cayenne to the kitchen appliance. Pulse until the material forms a course, coarse meal. Sometimes scrape the edges of the kitchen appliance.

- Place the mixture in a bowl, cool the flavors to cover and return together for 1-2 hours.

- Once cooled, remove from the refrigerator and make 1-inch inch balls, then flatten the balls a little.

- Heat the air to 400 degrees Fahrenheit. Lightly spray the fryer basket with oil.
- Place falafel in a basket, so that there is no overcrowding. Cook for 10 minutes, turning halfway through. Repeat with the remaining falafel.

Chapter 5: Air Fried Mediterranean Lunch Recipes

Air Fryer Fish and Fries

Ingredients

- 1-pound potato (about 2 medium)
- 2 tablespoons vegetable oil
- 1/4 teaspoon pepper
- 1/4 teaspoon salt

- Fish
- 1/3 cup all-purpose flour
- 1/4 teaspoon pepper
- 2 large eggs
- 2 tablespoons water
- 2/3 cup crushed cornflakes
- 1 tablespoon grated Parmesan cheese
- 1/8 teaspoon cayenne pepper
- 1/4 teaspoon salt
- 1-pound haddock or cod filters
- tartar sauce, alternate

Instructions

- Preheat the air fryer at 400 °. Peel and cut potatoes into 1/2-inch-thick slices; cut the slices into 1/2-in-thick sticks.
- In a large bowl, add potatoes with oil, pepper, and salt. Working in batches as needed, place potatoes during one layer in an air-fryer basket; Cook only until tender, 5–10 minutes to re-divide potatoes in baskets; Still light brown and crisp, cook for 5–10 minutes.
- Meanwhile, during a shallow bowl, mix flour and pepper. In another shallow bowl, whisk the egg with water. During a third bowl, toss corn flakes with cheese and cayenne. Sprinkle fish with salt; Dough mixture to read both sides;

Stir excess. Dip in egg mixture, then in the cornflake mixture, pat to aid adherence to coat.

- Remove the fries from the basket; To keep safe. Place the fish in a single layer in the fryer basket. Cook until the fish turns light brown and just starts to flourish easily with a fork, turning halfway through cooking. Do not overcook. Return the fries to heat through the basket. Serve immediately. If desired, serve with spicy chutney.

Cheese Egg Rolls

Ingredients

- 1/2-pound bulk sausage
- 1/2 cup chopped tart cheddar
- 1/2 cup chopped Monterey Jack cheese
- 1 tbsp chopped green onion

- 1 tbsp 2% milk
- 1/4 tsp salt
- 1/8 teaspoon black pepper
- 1 tablespoon butter
- 12 spring roll wrappers
- maple syrup or salsa, alternate

Instructions

- In a small nonstick pan, cooks the sausage over medium heat until it becomes pink, 4-6 minutes, breaking into pieces; drain. Stir in cheeses and green onions; put aside. Clean and wipe.
- In a small bowl, whisk eggs, milk, salt, and pepper. Within the same pan, heat the butter over medium heat. Pour in egg mixture; Cook and shake until the eggs thicken and no liquid egg remains. Stir in the sausage mixture.
- Preheat the air fryer at 400 degrees. With one corner of a spring roll wrapper, you place 1/4 cup slightly below the center of the wrapper. (Cover the remaining wrapper with a damp towel until able to use.) Fold the bottom corner over the filling; Moisten the remaining cover edges with water. Fold corners toward the center on filling. Roll the spring tightly, press on the tip to seal. Repeat
- In batches, arrange egg rolls during a crust on an increased tray in an air-fryer basket, Sprites with cooking spray.

Cook for 3-4 minutes until it becomes light brown. Turn, Sprites with cooking spray. Cook for 3-4 minutes until golden brown and crisp. Serve with syrup or salsa if desired.

Air Fryer Shrimp

Ingredients

- 1/2 cup mayonnaise
- 1 tbsp creole mustard
- 1 tbsp chopped cornichons or dill pickles
- 1 tbsp minced boiled
- 1/8 teaspoon cayenne pepper
- Coconut Shrimp

- 1 cup all-flour
- 1 teaspoon Herbs de Provence
- 1/2 teaspoon sea salt
- 1/2 teaspoon garlic powder
- 1/2 teaspoon pepper
- 1/4 teaspoon pepper black pepper
- 1 large egg
- 1/2 cup 2% milk
- 1 teaspoon hot onion
- cups sweetened shredded Nair Ripe.
- 1 pound uncooked (avid per pound), peeled and cooked hoagie
- cooking spray
- 4 buns,
- 2 cups of chopped lettuce
- 1 medium tomato, finely chopped

Instructions

- For remoulade, during a small bowl, add primary ingredients, Mix. Refrigerate, cover, serve until.
- Preheat the air fryer to 375 °. During a shallow bowl, mix flour, herbs de Provence, sea salt, garlic powder, black pepper, and cayenne. Whisk egg, milk, and warm poised during a separate shallow bowl. Place the coconut during the third shallow bowl. Dip the shrimp in flour to coat both

sides; Stir excess. Dip in egg mixture, then in coconut, pat to adhere.

- In batches, arrange the shrimp during one layer in an enlarged air-fryer basket; Sprites with cooking spray. Cook until the coconut turns light brown and the shrimp turns pink, 3-4 minutes on all sides.
- Spread the cut side of the buns with remoulade. Top with shrimp, lettuce and tomatoes.

Air Fryer Nashville Hot Chicken

Ingredients

- 2 tablespoons pickle juice, split, split
- 2 tablespoons hot plover peppers
- 1 teaspoon salt,
- 2 pounds chicken tenderloin
- 1 cup all-flour
- 1/2 teaspoon pepper 1/2
- 1 Large egg
- Half cup buttermilk

- Cooking Spray
- 1/2 cup vegetable oil
- 2 tablespoons cayenne pepper
- 2 tbsp dark sugar
- 1 teaspoon paprika
- 1 teaspoon flavor
- 1/2 teaspoon garlic powder
- Dill pickle slices

Instructions

- In a bowl or shallow dish, 1 tbsp Pickle juice, 1 tbsp sauce, and 1/2 teaspoon combine salt. Add chicken and switch to coat. Refrigerate, cover, minimum of 1 hour. Drain, discard pickles of any kind.
- Preheat the air fryer to 375 °. During a shallow bowl, mix flour, remaining 1/2 teaspoon salt and pepper. In another shallow bowl, whisk eggs, buttermilk, remaining 1 tbsp pickle juice and 1 tbsp sauce. To coat both sides of the chicken in flour; Stir excess. Dip in egg mixture, but flour mixture.
- In batches, arrange the chicken during a crust on a well-grown tray in an air-fryer basket, Sprites with cooking spray. Cook until golden brown, 5-6 minutes. Turn, Sprites with cooking spray. Cook for 5-6 minutes, until golden brown.

- Oil, cayenne pepper, sugar, and spice together; Pour hot chicken and toss to coat. Serve with Pickle

Air Fryer Crispy Spring Rolls

Ingredients

- 3 cups coleslaw mix (about 7 ounces)
- 3 green onions, chopped
- 1 tbsp soy
- 1 tablespoon vegetable oil
- 1-pound boneless chicken breasts

- skinless tsp flavor
- 2 packages (8 ounces each) cheese, softened
- 2 tablespoons) Sriracha Masala
- 24 egg roll wrappers
- cooking spray
- sweet masala, optional

Instructions

- Preheat the air fryer at 360 degrees. Toss Coleslaw mixture, green onion, soy and sesame oil; Stand while making chicken. Place the chicken in an increased air-fryer basket during a crust. Cook the thermometer inserted in the chicken for 165 °, 18-20 minutes. Remove Chicken; Little cool. Finely chopped chicken; Toss with flavor.
- Raise the air fryer temperature to 400 °. During a large bowl, combine cheese and Sriracha chili sauce; Stir in the chicken and coleslaw mixture. With one corner of the egg roll wrapper facing you, fill about 2 tablespoons under the center of the wrapper. (Cover the remaining wrapper with a damp towel until able to use.) Fold the bottom corner over the filling; Moisten the remaining edges with water. Fold corners toward the center on filling; Roll tightly, press the tip to seal. Repeat
- In batches, arrange spring rolls during one layer in an enlarged air-fryer basket; Sprites with cooking spray. Cook

until light brown, 5-6 minutes. Turn, Sprites with cooking spray. Cook for 5-6 minutes, until golden brown and crisp. If desired, serve with sweet spices.

- Freeze option: Freeze spring roll 1 of the freeze. Also, in freezer containers, separate the layers with wax paper. To use, cook frozen spring rolls as directed, extending time as needed.

Air Fryer Beef Swiss Bundles

Ingredients

- 1-pound hamburger
- 1/2 cups chopped fresh mushrooms
- 1/2 cup chopped onion
- 1/2 teaspoon minced garlic crushed
- 4 teaspoon Worcester sauce
- 3/4 teaspoon dried rosemary, Happened.
- 3/4 teaspoon paprika
- 1/2 teaspoon salt
- 1/4 teaspoon pepper
- 1 sheet frozen puff pastry, melted

- 2/3 cup refrigerated mashed potatoes
- 1 cup chopped swiss
- 2 tbsp water

Instructions

- Air from 375 ° Preheat Arya. During a large skillet, cook beef, mushrooms, and onions over medium heat until the meat is no longer pink, and the vegetables are tender, 8–10 minutes. Add garlic; cook 1 minute more. Stir in Worcester sauce and seasonings. Remove from heat; put aside.
- On a lightly puffed surface, roll the puff pastry 15x13-inches. Rectangle. Dig four 7-1 / 2x6-1 / 2-inch. Rectangles. Place about 2 tablespoons of potatoes over each rectangle; Spread to 1 of the edges. Top each with 3/4 cup beef mixture; sprinkle with 1/4 cup cheese.
- Beat egg and water; Brush some on the pastry edges. Bring opposite corners of the pastry above each bundle; Sew pinch to seal. Brush with the remaining egg mixture.
- In batches, place pastry during a single layer in an air-fryer basket; Cook for 10-12 minutes until golden brown.
- Freeze option: Stab the unbaked pastry on a parchment-lined baking sheet. Transfer to an airtight container; Return to the freezer. To use, direct the frozen pastry until

golden brown and warm it by increasing the time to 15-20 minutes.

Air Fryer Wasabi Crab

Ingredients

- 1 medium sweet red chili, finely chopped
- 1 celery rib, finely chopped
- 3 green onions, finely chopped
- 2 large egg whites
- 3 tablespoons low-fat mayonnaise
- 1/4 teaspoon prepared wasabi
- 1 / 4 teaspoons salt
- 1 /. 3 cups plus 1/2 cup dry breadcrumbs,

- 1/2 cups lump crab, dried
- Cooking spray

Sauce:

- 1 celery rib, sliced
- 1/3 cup low-fat mayonnaise
- 1 scallion, sliced
- 1 tablespoon pickle Troilus
- prepare the wasabi prepared by 1/2 teaspoon
- 1/4 teaspoon, preheat the

Instructions

- 375 degrees to fry. Spirit fryer basket with cooking spray. Combine the first 7 ingredients; add 1/3 cup breadcrumbs. Fold gently into the crab.
- Keep the remaining breadcrumbs during a shallow bowl. Spoon heaping crab mixture into the cramp. Gently coat and shape into a 3/4-inch-thick patty. Working in batches as needed, place the crab cakes during one layer in the basket. Spirit Crab Cake with Cooking Spray. Cook for 8–12 minutes until golden brown, carefully closing the cooking halfway point and spraying with additional cooking spray. Remove and keep warm. Repeat with remaining crab cakes.

- Meanwhile, place the sauce ingredients in the food processor; 2 or 3 times to mix the pulse or until the desired consistency is reached. Serve dip cake immediately with sauce.

Air Fryer Hamburger Wellington

Ingredients

- 1/2 cup chopped fresh mushrooms
- 1 tbsp butter
- 2 tablespoons all-purpose flour

- 1/4 teaspoon pepper, split
- 1/2 cup half and half cream
- 2 tbsp finely chopped onions
- 1/4 teaspoon salt
- 1/2-pound hamburger
- 1 tube (4 ounces) refrigerated crescent rolls
- 1 large egg, lightly beaten, optional
- 1 teaspoon flakes dried parsley

Instructions

- Preheat air300 degrees, Fryer. While in a saucepan, heat the butter over medium-high heat. Add mushrooms; cook and stir until tender, 5-6 minutes. Stir in the flour and 1/8 teaspoon pepper until mixed. Apply the cream slowly. Bring back a boil; cook and stir for two minutes or until thickened. Remove from heat and keep aside.
- In a bowl, combine ingredients, onion, 2 tablespoons sauce, salt and remaining 1/8 teaspoon pepper. Mixture and mix well-lacking beef. Shape into 2 loaves. Separate the crescent dough into 2 rectangles: Press holes to seal. Place meat bread on each rectangle. Bring the edges together and pinch to seal. If desired, brush with beaten egg.

- Place the Wellington in an enlarged air-fryer basket during a crust. Cook until golden brown and a thermometer inserted into the meatloaf reads 160 °, 18–22 minutes.
- Meanwhile, heat remaining sauce over low heat; Stir in parsley. Serve sauce with Wellington.

Air Fryer Loaded Pork Burritos

Ingredients

- 3/4 cup molten lime concentrate
- 1 tbsp vegetable oil
- 2 tablespoons salt
- 1/2 tablespoons pepper split divided
- 1-1/2 pounds of pork into the bonnet, thin strips
- 1 cup chopped seeds chopped. Plum tomatoes
- 1 small sweet chili,

- 1 small onion chopped,
- 1/4 cup plus 1/3 cup minced fresh
- 1 jalapeno, seeds and sliced uncooked
- 1 tbsp juice
- 1/4 teaspoon powder
- 1 cup of rice
- 2 cups of sliced Monterey Jack Cheese
- 6 flour tortillas (12 in), hot
- 1 can (15 oz) black beans, rinsed and drained
- 1/2 cups sour cream
- cooking spray

Instructions

- Limed concentrate, in a large shallow dish Oil, 1 combine teaspoon salt and 1/2 teaspoon pepper; add pork. Address quote: Cover and refrigerate for at least 20 minutes.
- For salsa, during a small bowl, combine tomatoes, sweet peppers, onions, 1/4 cup ditophal, jalapeno, juice, garlic powder, and the remaining salt and pepper.
- Meanwhile, cook rice as per package instructions. Stir in the remaining cilantro; To keep safe.
- Drain pork, discard pickles. Preheat the air fryer to 350 degrees in batches and place pork in a single air-fryer basket during a single layer; Sprites with cooking spray. Cook until the pork is pink, 8-10 minutes, turning halfway.

- Sprinkle 1/3 cup of cheese off-center on each tortilla. Mix each with 1/4 cup salsa, 1/2 cup rice mixture, 1/4 cup black beans and 1/4 cup sour cream, about 1/2 cup pork. Fill the sides and ends on the filling. Serve with the remaining salsa.

Air Fryer Green Tomato

Ingredients

- 2 medium green tomatoes (about 10 ounces)
- 1/2 teaspoon salt
- 1/4 teaspoon pepper

- 1 large egg, beaten
- 1/4 cup all-purpose flour
- 1 cup panko breadcrumbs
- Cooking spray
- 1 / 2 cups low-fat mayonnaise
- 2 green onions, finely chopped
- 1 teaspoon fresh dill or 1/4 teaspoon dilute,
- 8 slices toasted whole wheat bread
- 8 cooked centers cut bacon strips
- 4 Bibb or Boston salad leaves

Instructions

- 350 Preheat air Fryer °. Cut each tomato bowl into 4 slices. Sprinkle it with salt and pepper. Put eggs, flour, and breadcrumbs in separate shallow bowls. Dip the tomato slices in the flour, shaking off the excess, then read the eggs, and finally tap into the bread crumb mixture to adhere.

- In batches, arrange tomato slices during a crust on an increased tray in an air-fryer basket, Sprites with cooking spray. Cook for 4-6 minutes until golden brown. Turn, Sprites with cooking spray. Cook for 4-6 minutes until golden brown.

- Meanwhile, combine mayonnaise, green onion, and dill. Layer each of the 4 slices of bread with 2 bacon strips, 1 salad leaf and a couple of tomato slices. Spread mayonnaise mixture over remaining slices of bread, Place from above. serve immediately.

Air Fryer Tortellini with Prosciutto

Ingredients

- 1 tablespoon vegetable oil
- 3 tablespoons finely chopped onion
- 4 garlic cloves, coarsely chopped
- 1 can (15 ounces) tomato puree
- 1 tbsp minced fresh basil

- 1/4 teaspoon salt
- 1 / 4 teaspoon pepper
- Tortellini:
- 2 large eggs
- 2 tablespoons 2% milk
- 2/3 cup spice breadcrumbs
- 1 teaspoon garlic powder
- 2 tablespoons grated Pecorino Romano cheese
- 1 tablespoon fresh parsley
- 1/2 teaspoon salt
- 1 packaging (12 ounces) refrigerated Prosciutto Ricotta Tortellini
- cooking spray

Instructions

- Heat in a small saucepan. Oil over medium-high heat. Add onion and garlic; cook and stir until tender, 3-4 minutes. Stir in tomato puree, basil, salt, and pepper. Bring back a boil; warm down. Simmer, open, 10 minutes. To keep safe.
- Meanwhile, preheat the air fryer to 350 °. During a small bowl, egg, and milk. In another bowl, combine breadcrumbs, garlic powder, cottage cheese, parsley, and salt.
- Dip the Angelina in the egg mixture, then coat it in the bread crumb mixture. In batches, arrange tortellini during

one layer in an enlarged air-fryer basket; Sprites with cooking spray. Cook 4-5 minutes until golden brown. Turn, Sprites with cooking spray. Cook for 4-5 minutes, until golden brown. Serve with Sauce, Sprinkle with additional minced fresh basil.

Air Fryer Herb and Cheese-Stuffed Burger

Ingredients

- 2 green onions, finely chopped
- 2 tablespoons fresh parsley
- 4 tablespoons mustard,
- daejon3 tablespoons dry breadcrumbs
- 2 tablespoons ketchup

- 1/2 teaspoon salt
- 1/2 teaspoon dried Henna, crushed Hochmuth.
- 14 teaspoon dried sage leaves
- 1-pound lean hamburger (90% lean)
- 2 ounces cheddar, sliced
- 4 hamburger buns, split
- Optional toppings: lettuce, sliced tomatoes, mayonnaise, and extra ketchup

Instructions

- Air Fryer preheat to 375 °. During a small bowl, combine a pair of green onions, parsley and a tablespoon of mustard. In another bowl, add breadcrumbs, ketchup, seasonings and the remaining 2 tablespoons of mustard. Add beef to the bread crumb mixture; mix lightly but well.
- Shape mixture into 8 thin patties. Place sliced cheese in the center of 4 patties; Spoon mixture over cheese. Top with the remaining patties, taking care to seal them completely, pressing the edges firmly.
- Place the burger during a crust in an air-fryer basket. Working in batches as required, air-fry 8 minutes; flip and continue cooking until the thermometer reads 160 °, 6-8 minutes longer. Serve burgers on buns with toppings if desired.

Air Fryer Turkey Croquettes

Ingredients

- 2 cups mashed potatoes (with added milk and butter)
- 1/2 cup grated cheese
- 1/2 cup chopped Swiss cheese
- 1 onion, finely chopped

- 2 tablespoons minced fresh henna or 1/2 teaspoon dry henna, crushed
- 1 teaspoon minced fresh sage or 1/4 teaspoon dried sage leaves
- 1/2 teaspoon salt
- 1/4 teaspoon pepper
- 3 cups finely chopped cooked turkey
- 2 tbsp water
- 1 -1 / 4 Panko Bread Crumb This
- Butter-Flavor Cooking Spray
- Sour. Cream, alternate

Instructions

- Heat the air floor to 350 °. During a large bowl, combine the mashed potatoes, cottage cheese, shallot, rosemary, sage, salt, and pepper; Stir in turkey. Twelve 1-in.-thick patties in size.
- In a shallow bowl, whisk eggs and water. Place the breadcrumbs in another shallow bowl. Dip the crisps in the egg mixture, then pat in the breadcrumbs to aid adherence to the coating.
- In batches, place croquettes during a single layer in a Greer fryer basket; Sprites with cooking spray. Cook 4-5 minutes until golden brown. Turn, Sprites with cooking spray.

Cook until golden brown; 4-5 minutes. If desired, serve with sour cream.

Air Fryer Bourbon Bacon Cinnamon Rolls

Ingredients

- 8 bacon strips
- 3/4 cup bourbon
- 1 tube (12.4 oz) refrigerated cinnamon rolls
- 1/2 cup chopped pecans
- 2 tablespoons syrup
- 1 tablespoon minced fresh ginger root

Instructions

- Place bacon during shallow dish; Add bourbon. Seal and refrigerate overnight. Remove bacon and pat dry; Discard the burbs.

- In a large pan, baking bacon in batches over medium heat is almost crisp but still viable. Remove paper towels to empty. Discard about 1 teaspoon of drippings.

- Preheat the air fryer to 350 degrees. Separate the dough into 8 rolls, burning the icing packet. Unscrew the spiral rolls into long strips; 6x1-in to make the pat dough. Strips. Place 1 bacon on each strip of flour, trimming the bacon as needed: Formation of the spiral. Pinch ends to seal. Repeat with remaining flour. Transfer 4 rolls to the air-fryer basket; Cook for 5 minutes. Turn the rolls over and cook for about 4 minutes until they turn golden brown.

- Meanwhile, mix pecans and syrup. In another bowl, shake the ginger with the contents of the icing packet. In the same pan, heat remaining bacon dripping over medium heat. Add pecan mixture; Cook, frequently stirring until lightly fry, 2-3 minutes.

- Drizzle half the pieces on a hot cinnamon roll; Top with half the pecans. Repeat to make a second batch.

Air Fryer Coconut Shrimp and Sauce

Ingredients

- 1/2 pounds Large Shrimp
- 1/2 Cups Sweet Sliced Coconut
- 1/2 cup Panko Breadcrumbs
- 4 Large Egg Whites

- Dashes Louisiana-Style Sauce
- 1/4 Spoon Salt
- 1/4 teaspoon pepper
- 1/2 cup all-purpose flour

Instructions

- Preheat the air 375 ° Fryer. Peel and Devin are leaving the shrimp on the tail.
- In a shallow bowl, toss the coconut with the breadcrumbs. In another shallow bowl, whisk egg whites, hot sauce, salt, and pepper. Place the dough during the third shallow bowl.
- To lightly coat shrimp in flour; Stir excess. Dip in albumen mixture, then in coconut mixture, pat to aid adherence of coating.
- Spray the fryer basket with cooking spray. Working in batches as needed, place the shrimp in the basket during a single layer. Cook for 4 minutes; Turn the shrimp on and continue cooking until the coconut turns light brown and the shrimp turns pink another 4 minutes.
- Meanwhile, combine sauce ingredients during a small saucepan; Cook and shake over medium-low heat until preserved. Serve shrimp immediately with chutney.

Air Fryer Quentin-Bourbon Feather

Ingredients

- 1/2 cup peach retains
- 1 tbsp sugar
- 1 garlic clove, minced
- 1/4 tsp salt
- 2 tbsp white vinegar
- 2 tbsp bourbon
- 1 tsp cornstarch

- 1/2 tablespoons water
- pounds of chicken wings

Instructions

- Preheat the air fryer at 400 degrees. Preserve sugar, garlic and salt during the food processor, process until blended. Transfer to a little saucepan. Add vinegar and bourbon; Bring back a boil. Warm down; Boil, uncovered, until slightly thickened, 4-6 minutes.
- In a small bowl, mix cornstarch and water until smooth; Stir in the preserved mixture. Return to a boil, stirring constantly; Cook for 1-2 minutes or until thickened. Reserve 1/4 cup sauce for serving.
- Using a sharp knife, cut back 2 joints on each chicken wing: Discard wing tips. Spray the air fryer basket with cooking spray. Working in batches as needed, place the wing pieces during one layer in the air fryer basket. Cook for 6 minutes; turn and brush with preserved mixture. Return to the air fryer and cook until it turns brown and the juices run clear for 6-8 minutes. Remove and keep warm. Repeat with the remaining wing pieces. Serve the wings immediately with reserved chutney.

Chapter 6: Air Fried Mediterranean Snack Recipes

Air Fryer Pizza

Ingredients

- Buffalo Mozzarella
- Pizza Dough 1 12 Inch Dough Will Make 2 Individual Size Pizza
- Olive Oil
- Tomato Sauce

- Optional Topping: Fresh Basil, Parmesan Cheese, Pepper Seeds to Finish

Instructions

- Prep: Preheat air fryer to 375 ° F (190 ° C)). Thoroughly spray the air fryer basket with oil. Pat mozzarella dries with paper towels (to prevent a disgusting pizza).
- Assemble: Roll the pizza dough to the dimensions of your air fryer basket. Carefully transfer it to the air fryer, then brush it lightly with about a teaspoon of vegetable oil. Spoon over a light layer of spaghetti sauce and sprinkle with a slice of buffalo mozzarella.
- Bake: for about 7 minutes until the crust is crispy and the cheese is melted. Alternately top with basil, grated Parmesan, and pepper flakes before serving.

Air Fried Vegetables

Ingredients

- Tender Vegetables
- Crucifers Broccoli, Cauliflower, Brussels Sprouts Like
- Capsicum, Veggies, Tomato
- Asparagus LinkedIn
- Firm Vegetables
- Root Vegetable Carrots, Beets, Potatoes, Beet
- Winter Squash Butternut, Acorn, Pumpkin
- Frozen vegetables

Instructions

- 375 degrees F (190 C) to preheat the air fryer to tender Sibson Jiu. Veggies by chopping them to your preferred dimensions, alternately dripping with oil (this will give them a more frying edge within the end Will taste) Raise your air fryer in as flat of a layer as possible and cook for 10 to fifteen minutes, cooking in the market even while shaking the air fryer pan once or twice while cooking.

- Firm veggie: 375 degrees F (190 C) to preheat air fryer. Prepare them by cutting them to your preferred dimensions (remember small pieces cook faster!) Dripping alternately with oil and raising your air fryer in as flat of a layer as possible. Cook for 20 to half an hour, keep the air fryer pan shaking for some time while cooking, even for cooking.

- Frozen Vegetables: Find out which category your vegetable falls under (see tender or firm, see the note above), then add a few minutes to the cooking time to account for the melting vegetables during the cooking process. Make sure they offer space between your vegetables to be fully roasted.

Baked General Tso's Cauliflower

Ingredients

- Cauliflower
- Half-Head Cauliflower
- Half-Cup Dough
- 2 Large Eggs

- 60gTransported 1 Cup Panko Breadcrumbs 50g15ml
- ¼ Spoon Each Salt and Pepper
- General Tso's Sauce
- 1 Gourd Vegetable Oil
- 2 Cloves Garlic Minced
- 1 Gourd Fresh grated ginger
- ½ cup vegetable broth 120 mL
- soy cup soy 60 mL
- vine cup rice vinegar 60 mL
- sugar cup sugar 50 grams
- 2 tons 2 tablespoons 30
- tablespoons cornstarch 2 tablespoons (30 mA) L) 15 gin cold water

Instructions

- Prep: 400 ° F (204) ° C in a preheated oven) *. Arrange the workspace by placing flour, egg, and panko in separate bowls. Add salt and pepper to the poncho. Cut the cabbage into bite-sized flowers.
- Dredge: Working in batches, coat the florets in flour, then egg, then breadcrumbs. Combine parchment paper-lined baking sheets. Bake for 15 to 20 minutes, or until crispy.
- Sauce: Set a little saucepan over medium heat and add vegetable oil, garlic, and ginger. Cook two minutes until fragrant, then add the remaining sauce ingredients,

leaving the cornstarch mixture. Mix and boil. While whisking, slowly pour within the cornstarch mixture. It should thicken quite quickly; If not, keep boiling until thick.

- Assemble: Drizzle sauce over the cooked cabbage and toss gently to coat evenly. Serve cauliflower over hot rice or quinoa.

Crispy Baked Avocado Tacos

Ingredients

- 1 cup finely chopped or crushed pineapple 240 grams
- Romana 1 tomato finely chopped
- 1/2 red pepper, finely chopped
- 1/2 medium Purple onion 1/2 cup, finely. Chopped

- 1 clove minced garlic
- 1/2 jalapeno finely chopped
- pinch of cumin and salt
- avocado tacos
- 1 advocator
- 1/4 cup alate 35 grams
- 1 large egg
- whipped 1/2 cup pence crabs 65 grams
- pinch each salt and black Chili
- 4 Maida Tortilla Click for recipe
- Adobo Sauce
- 1/4 cup plain yogurt 60 grams
- 2 Karachi mayonnaise 30 grams
- 1/4 teaspoon juice
- Chipotle pepper 1 Karachi adobo sauce from a jar

Instructions

- Salsa: All Salsa Ingredients (Patel Combine processor sliced by hand or blitz within the food), cover, and set in the fridge.
- Prep Avocado: Cut the avocado in half lengthwise and remove the pit. Put the avocado skin down and cut each half into 4 equal size pieces, then gently peel off the skin.
- Prep Station: Preheat oven to 450 F (230 C) or 375 F (190 C) to air fryer. Arrange your workspace so that you get a

bowl of flour, a bowl of whisked eggs, a bowl of Panko with S&P and a parchment-lined baking sheet on top.

- Coat: Dip each piece of avocado first within the flour, then egg, then panko. Place on a prepared baking sheet and bake or air fry for 10 minutes, half-cooked until lightly cooked.

- Sauce: While the avocados are cooking, mix all the sauce ingredients.

- Serve: Spoon salsa on a tortilla, drizzle with 2 pieces of avocado and sauce. Serve immediately and enjoy!

Baked Potatoes

Instructions

- Cake Air Fryer Prep: Preheat air fryer to 390 degrees F (200 C). Rub the potatoes with a little oil and sprinkle with salt.

- Cook: Set the potatoes within the air fryer during the same layer. Cook for 30 to 45 minutes, or until fork-tender, flip them once while cooking to cook evenly.

- air fryer french-fried potatoes

- Soak the: With the help of a matchstick or knife, break the potato or cut it into a mandolin slicer. Soak sliced potatoes in a bowl of cold water for 1 to 2 hours. This removes the starch to offer them a completely crispy texture!

- Prep: Preheat air fryer to 390 degrees F (200 C). Dry and pat dry potatoes. Increase a bowl, then drizzle with oil (about 1 teaspoon per potato) and a pinch of salt.
- Cook: Add fries to your air fryer, opened as crusted as possible. Cook for 15 to twenty minutes, stirring the basket once or twice while cooking evenly.

Air Fryer Potato Chips

Instructions

- Cut the potatoes thinly using a knife or mandolin slicer. Soak sliced potatoes in a bowl of cold water for 1 to 2 hours. With a little bit of air fryer potato fry, it removes the starch to make it completely crisp.

- Prep: Preheat the air fryer to 300 degrees F (150 C). Dry and pat dry potatoes. Increase a bowl, then drizzle with oil (about 1 teaspoon per potato) and a pinch of salt.

- Cook: Add potatoes to your air fryer, open as crust as possible. Cook for 20 to half an hour, shake the basket once or twice to cook evenly. (If you hear your chips flying within the air fryer, you will cover them with your air fryer grill plate to keep them relatively in place.)

Buttermilk Fried Mushroom

Ingredients

- 2 Heating Cups Oyster Mushrooms
- 1 Cup Buttermilk 240 See notes for ML, vegetarian options.
- 1 1/2 cups all-purpose flour 200 grams
- 1 tsp each salt, pepper, garlic powder, onion powder, smoked paprika, cumin

Instructions

- Kettle Marinette: Preheat air to 375 degrees F (190 C). During a large bowl, clean the mushrooms with buttermilk. Marinate for quarter hours.

- Breaking: Combine flour and spices during a large bowl. Spoon mushrooms out of the buttermilk (save the buttermilk). Dip each mushroom within the flour mixture, shake off the excess flour, one more time within the buttermilk, then another time within the dough (briefly: wet> dry> wet> dry).

- Cook: Stir the rock well under your air fry pan, then place the mushrooms during a single layer, leaving space between the mushrooms. Cook for five minutes, then brush all sides with a touch of oil for browning. Continue to cook for 5 to 10 minutes until golden brown and crispy.

Chapter 7: Air Fried Mediterranean Dinner Recipes

Air Fryer Blacken Fish Tacos

Ingredients

- Fryer Blacken Fish Tacos 1 (15 oz)
- Seeds Beans, Rinsed and Drenched
- 2 Year Corn,

- 1 Tablespoon Vegetable Oil
- 1 Tablespoon Juice
- 1/2 Spoon Salt
- 1 Pound Tilapia Fillets
- Cooking Spray
- 1/4 Cup Blackening Seasoning
- 4 Corn tortillas
- 1 lime
- 1 teaspoon Louisiana style sauce (optional)

Instructions

- Preheat the oven to 400 ° F (200 ° C).
- Combine black beans, corn, olive oil, lemon juice, and salt during a bowl. Gently stir until beans and corn are evenly coated; put aside.
- Lay the fish fillet on a clean surface and pat it with paper towels. Lightly sprinkle each fillet with cooking spray and sprinkle 1/2 of black pepper over the top. Flip the faults, spray with cooking spray, and sprinkle with the remaining seasonings.
- If necessary, place the fish during a crust within the basket of the air fryer working in batches. Cook for two minutes. Flip the fish over and cook for 2 more minutes, Transfer to a plate.

- Place the bean and corn mixture in the air fryer basket and cook for 10 minutes, stirring halfway through.
- Place the fish with a mixture of corn tortilla and bean and corn. Serve with lime wedges and sauce.

Air Fryer Coconut Chicken

Ingredients

- ½ cup of canned coconut milk
- ½ cup fruit juice
- 2 tablespoons sugar
- 1 tbsp soy

- 2 tablespoons Sriracha sauce
- 1 tablespoon ground ginger
- 1-pound boneless skinless chicken breasts, digging strips
- 2 eggs
- 1 cup coconut chopped sweet
- 1 cup panko bread Pieces of
- ½ teaspoon salt
- spoon ground black pepper
- easy nonstick cooking spray

Instructions

Step 1: Take a medium-sized bowl and coconut milk in the mix Whisk, fruit juice, sugar, soy sauce, Sriracha sauce, and ginger. Add chicken strips and toss to coat. Cover with wrapping and refrigerate for 2 hours or overnight.

Step 2: Preheat an air fryer to 375 degrees F (190 degrees C).

Step 3: Whisk eggs during a bowl. In a separate bowl mix chopped coconut, panko, salt, and pepper.

Step 4: Remove chicken strips from the pickle and shake off excess. Discard the remaining pickles. Dip the chicken strips in the beaten egg, then in the coconut-panko mixture, but again in the egg mixture, and again in the coconut-panko mixture, each strip income and double coating.

Step 5: Spray the air fryer basket with cooking spray.

Step 6: Place the braided chicken strips within the air fryer basket, making sure they are not touching; Add batch if necessary.

Step 7: Cook for six minutes, beat the strips, and cook until lightly brown and toasted, 4 to six minutes more.

Air Fryer Salmon Patties

Ingredients

- 12 oz salmon minced
- 1 tbsp peeled fresh chives
- 1 tablespoon dried Parsley with 1 teaspoon finely spoon powder.

- Tablespoon all-purpose flour, or as needed,
- 1 lemon
- Cooking spray

Aioli Dipping Sauce:

- 1/2 cup mayonnaise
- 1 teaspoon finely minced garlic
- 1/2 teaspoon fresh juice
- 2 pinch cousin seasoning papaya

Instructions

- Mayonnaise, garlic, lemon juice, and Cajun seasoning mix together during a small bowl and dip sauce until needed.
- Keep salmon, chives, parsley, garlic, and salt in a medium bowl and mix well. Add flour and mix well. Divide into 4 equal parts: Mold in patties.
- Preheat the air fryer to 350 degrees F (175 degrees C). Cut the lemon into 4 slices.
- Place slices of lemon in the bottom of the air fryer basket and salmon patties on top. Lightly spray patty with cooking spray.
- Place the basket in a preheated fryer and leave the temperature up to 275 degrees F (135 degrees C).

- Cook within the air fryer until an instant-read thermometer inserted in the middle of a patty reads 145 ° F (63 ° C), 10 to fifteen minutes. Serve with sauce.

Breaded Air Fryer Pork Chops

Ingredients

- 4 boneless, center-cut pork chops, 1-inch thick
- 1 tablespoon Cajun seasoning
- 1 cheese cup cheese and garlic-flavored croutons
- 2 eggs

Instructions

Step 1: Air fryer to 390 ° F (200 ° C).

Step 2: Place the pork chops on a plate and sew each side with Cajun masala.

Step 3: Pulse croutons during small kitchen appliances until they require fine stability, Transfer to a shallow dish. Lightly beat eggs during a separate shallow dish. Dip the pork chops into the egg, closing excess drip. Bread chopping and a plate assail in coat crouton. Mist Chop with Cooking Spray.

Step 4: Spray the basket of the air fryer with cooking spray and place the choppers inside, so as not to uproot the fryer. You will need to calculate two batches on the dimensions of your air fryer.

Step 5: Cook for five minutes. If there is a dry or powdery area, chop again with a cooking spray and add mist. Cook for another 5 minutes. Repeat with remaining chops.

Air Fryer BBQ Ribs

Ingredients

- 1 Rack
- 1 Tbsp Olive Oil
- 1 Tbsp Liquid Smoke Flavor
- 1 Tablespoon Sugar

- ½ Tablespoon Salt
- Tablespoon Pepper
- Powdered Tablespoon Garlic Powder
- ½ Tablespoons Onion Powder
- ½ Tablespoons Flavors

Instructions

Step 1: Remove the membrane from the back ribs and dry ribs with a towel. Cut the rack into 4 pieces. Combine vegetable oil and liquid smoke in a small bowl and rub each side of the ribs.

Step 2: Add sugar, salt, pepper, garlic powder, onion powder and flavor during a bowl. Season each side of the ribs liberally with the seasoning mix. Let the ribs rest for half an hour to strengthen the taste.

Step 3: Preheat an air fryer to 375 degrees F (190 degrees C).

Step 4: Place the rib bone under the air fryer basket, ensuring that they are not touching; Cook in batches if necessary.

Step 5: Cook for quarter-hours. Flip the ribs (meat-side down) and cook for 10 minutes. Remove the ribs from the air fryer and brush the ribs bone-side with 1/2 cup BBQ sauce. Place the basket inside the air fryer and cook for five minutes. Flip the ribs, brushing the meat-side with the remaining 1/2 cup of BBQ sauce; cook a further 5 minutes or until desired char is achieved.

Mexican-Style Air Fryer Stuffed Chicken Breast

Ingredients

- 4 extra-long toothpicks
- 4 teaspoons flavored
- 4 teaspoons ground cumin,
- 1 skinless, boneless pigeon breasts

- 2 teaspoons flakes
- 2 teaspoons Mexican oregano
- salt and ground black pepper to taste
- all red bell pepper, onion, into thin strips
- chopped thin strips
- 1 fresh Jalapeno, sliced into thin strips
- 2 tablespoons vegetable oil time Chon

Instructions

Step 1: Toothpicks during canopy with a small bowl and water. Allow them to soak during cooking to prevent them from burning.

Step 2: Combine 2 teaspoons of flavor and one or two teaspoons of cumin during a shallow dish.

Step 3: Preheat an air fryer to 400 ° F (200 ° C).

Step 4: Place the pigeon breast on a flat surface. Slice horizontally through the center. Use a kitchen mallet or kitchen utensil about half / 4-inch thick.

Step 5: Sprinkle each breast evenly in half with the remaining flavor, remaining cumin, chipotle flakes, parsley, salt, and pepper. Place 1/2 bell pepper, onion and jalapeno within the center of 1 breast half. Roll the chicken upside down from the taped end and use 2 toothpicks to secure. Repeat with other breasts, spices and vegetables and secure with remaining toothpicks. Drizzle with vegetable oil until evenly covered, roll each roll within the chili-cumin mixture within a shallow dish.

Step 6: Place the roll-up inside the air-fryer basket, which has a side portion of a toothpick. Set a timer for six minutes.

Step 7: Continue cooking within the air fryer until the juices run clear and an instantaneous read thermometer inserted in the middle reads at a minimum of 165 ° F (74 ° C), about 5 minutes.

Step 8: Juice evenly on roll-up before serving.

Air Fryer Beef Wellington

Ingredients

- Air fryer Grill Pan
- Knife Sharpener
- Cling Film
- Homemade Liver Pate
- Homemade Shortcrust Pastry
- Beef
- 1 Medium Beaton Egg
- Salt & Piper

Instructions

- Get your Beef Sawdust clean it with Salt and Salt in Any Weather Cut it. Pepper then seal it with cling film and keep it inside the fridge for an hour.
- Make your batch of Lever Pete and Homemade Shortcrust Pastries.
- Roll your shortcrust pastry and employ a pastry brush and round the edges with the beaten egg to make it sticky for sealing.
- Then place a thin layer of homemade peat inside the outer egg line until you see white pastry.
- Remove the cling film from the meat and place the meat on top of the peat and push it down a touch.
- Meat and, therefore, peat pastry.
- Gives the meat a chance to breathe, score the highest of the pastries in that order.
- Place the air fryer on the grill pan within the air fryer and cook for 35 minutes at 160c / 320f.
- Leave to rest for a few minutes, slice and serve with roasted potatoes.

Notes:

It is easy to pre-make pastries to save on time and, therefore, already create within the day. I do a full batch of both my pastry recipe and my peat recipe. Then whatever remains are often used later.

Then fridge them both for an hour, then they become easy to handle. If you want to cheat and make it appear as if it is puff pastry, make my shortcrust pastry, but swap dough for your dough.

Easy Air Fryer Pizza

Ingredients

- 1 Whole Wheat Patina
- 2 Tablespoon Pizza Sauce or Marinara If you don't like a thick sauce, you can make 1 tablespoon
- 1/8 cup of mozzarella cheese, sliced

- 1/8 cup of cheddar, if you only use mozzarella Flavored cheese, omit and use 1/4th cup mozzarella
- 8 slices pepperoni
- olive oil spray
- 1 teaspoon chopped parsley, for pizza garnish when it is cooled Alternative

Instructions

Standard Nerdish:

- Sauce on top of pita bread drizzle, then cheese Tar pepperoni Lod war.
- Mostly, spray the pizza with vegetable oil spray.
- Keep within an air fryer for 8 minutes at 400 degrees. Sign up on the pizza at the 6-7-minute mark to make sure it is not to your liking.
- Remove pizza from the air fryer. I used a spatula. Refrigerate before serving.

Crispy Crust:

- To have a crisper crust, spray one side of the beaten bread with vegetable oil. Keep inside the air fryer at 400 degrees for 4 minutes. It can be completely crisp from one side.
- Remove the beaten bread from the air fryer. Turn the pyre on the side, which is less crisp. This could be the side that was face-down within the air fryer.

- Drizzle all over the chutney, then load pepperoni and chopped cheese on top.

- Place the pizza back within the air fryer for 3-4 minutes until the cheese is frying. Use your judgment. This will allow you to cook the pizza for a few more minutes to succeed in its essential texture.

- Remove pizza from the air fryer. I used a spatula. Refrigerate before serving.

Quinoa Air Fried Burger

Ingredients

- 1 cup quinoa red, white or multi-colored
- 1½ cups water
- 1 tablespoon salt
- fresh pepper
- 1½ cups oatmeal or wheat breadcrumbs
- 3 eggs lightly beaten
- ¼ cup white onion minced
- ½ cup cheese broken

- ¼ cup chopped fresh chives
- salt and freshly ground pepper,
- vegetable or vegetable oil
- 4 wheat Hamburger Ns
- 4 arugulas
- chopped HeartMate 4 slices
- cucumber yogurt dill sauce
- 1 cup Kody Sushmita chopped
- 1 cup Grid
- 2 f Mc
- ¼ teaspoon
- Salt
- Fresh black juice
- 1 tbsp fresh dill chopped
- 1 tbsp vegetable Tel Kino

Instructions

- Make during saucepan quinoa, rinse in cold water, it rotates together with your hands until a dry husk is not the surface Go Also dry the quinoa as you will place the saucepan on the stovetop. Turn the heat to medium-high and dry the quinoa on the stovetop, shaking the pan regularly until you see the quinoa moving easily and the seeds occupying the pan. Add water, salt, and pepper. Bring liquid to a boil then reduce heat to medium-low. You just want to see a couple of bubbles, not a boil. Cover with the lid, leaving it sequel (or if you put a spout, just put the lid on the pot) and boil for 20 minutes. Turn off the heat and inflate the quinoa with a fork. If there is any liquid left inside the bottom of the pot, put it back on the burner for about 3 minutes. Spread the cooked quinoa on a sheet pan to cool.

- Combine space temperature quinoa during a large bowl with oats, eggs, onions, cheese, and herbs. Season with salt and pepper and mix well. Shape the mixture into 4 patties. Add a touch of water or an addition of more oatmeal to urge the mixture to be the proper consistency to make the patty.
- Spray each side of the patties generously with oil and transfer them to the basket of the air fryer in one layer (you will need to cook these burgers in a count on the dimensions of your air fryer). Air-fry, each batch at 400°F for 10 minutes, flipping more than half the burgers through the cooking time.

- While the burgers are cooking, make a cucumber curd sauce by mixing all the ingredients during a bowl.
- Build your burger on whole-wheat hamburger buns with arugula, tomato and so cucumber yogurt sauce.

Air Fried Unsaturated Veggies

Ingredients

- Vegan Stuffed 2 Large Idaho / Russet Baking Potatoes Unsaturated Veg
- 1 to 2 Tablespoons of Vegetable Oil Leave Oil to Make Free,
- 1/4 Cupcake
- 1/4 Cup Non-Dairy Milk

- 2 Tbsp Nutritional Yeast
- 1 /. 2 teaspoons salt subforum salt-free for your favorite salt-free
- 1/4 teaspoon pepper
- 1 cup chopped spinach or cabbage
- optional Topping Ingredients:
- 1/4 cup sweet vegetarian yogurt
- smoked salt and pepper
- chopped chives parsley or other favorite fresh herbs Bootie

Instructions

- Rub each potato with oil on all sides.
- Preheat your air fryer to 390 ° until your model requires it. Once it is hot, put the potato in the basket of your air fryer.
- Set the cooking time to half an hour and when it's time, flip the potatoes and cook for 30 minutes.
- Note: Depending on the dimensions of your potato, you will need to cook for 10 to 20 minutes ahead. You will know that once they are ready, you can easily pierce it with a fork.
- Let the potatoes cool enough that you can touch them without burning yourself.
- Cut each potato in half lengthwise and sieve the center of the potato periodically, leaving enough to form a thin layer of potato peel and white portion.

- Mash the scooped potatoes, veg curd, non-dairy milk, nutritional yeast, salt, and pepper until smooth.
- Stir within the chopped spinach and fill the potato shells with the mixture.
- Depending on the dimensions of your air fryer, you will be ready to cook all 4 parts at once; otherwise, you may need to cook 2 of them at once.
- Cook at 350 degrees for five minutes (or set that often as close as your air fryer).
- Serve with the topping options of your choice and enjoy!

Conclusion

Thank you for making it through to the end of Mediterranean Diet Air Fryer Cookbook, let's hope it was informative and able to provide you with all of the tools you need to achieve your goals whatever they may be.

The objective of this guide is to help you discover all the benefits and alternatives of preparing Mediterranean Diet meals to easily learn how to prepare and plan healthy and balanced meals for every day of the week and to start saving time, money, calories, and energy!

We also hope you will find the recipes we shared with you useful and enjoyable, on how to plan a balanced breakfast, lunch, and dinner quickly and easily for the whole family.

Finally, if you found this book useful in any way, a review is always appreciated!

CPSIA information can be obtained
at www.ICGtesting.com
Printed in the USA
LVHW080033011220
673086LV00058B/2942